Til Death
Do Us Part

By Emilee Hines

Til Death Do Us Part

by

Emilee Hines

Copyright 2011 ©Emilee Hines Cantieri

Cover and interior design by Catherine Cantieri

INTRODUCTION

You meet, you fall in love, you marry and have many good years together. You share your lives, your home, your children and your futures. You've loved each other so long that it feels like you've been together forever and always will be together forever. But "forever" isn't a concept that's possible for human lifetimes.

One moment, you're a happy couple; in the next, one of you dies and the other is left to go on alone. You'll face a mass of legal, financial, emotional and practical tasks at a time when you are most vulnerable and least able to make sound decisions. Are you ready?

Nothing can erase the inevitability of death or the grief that follows, but what you do now can make the months and years afterward more serene and secure. And your present relationship will be stronger because of it.

Young couples can benefit from this guidebook as much as older readers, for death can come at any age.

There are thousands of books on estate planning, funeral planning, organizing and dealing with grief, but *Til Death Do Us Part* is unique in covering both before and after a spouse's death. Most of my suggestions are things that any couple can do at little or no cost, except for having legal documents prepared by an attorney.

I'm not a legal or financial expert or a grief counselor. I relate what worked for me and for others when we were widowed, and in some cases, what we wish we'd known or done.

Some of my sources asked that I not use their real names, and I have honored their wishes, using pseudonyms or in some cases first names only. Several others wanted their full names noted, and I have honored their wishes as well.

The most loving gift you can give your spouse is not an expensive watch or ring or any other material thing, but trust and peace of mind. Reading and discussing Til Death Do Us Part and following through on the practical suggestions included doesn't mean you are fixated on death. Rather, it means that you recognize the inevitable and want to do what is best for your spouse after your death, or for yourself. Either of you could be the survivor.

We prepare for vacations, for surgery, for a move to a new home, for weddings, childbirth and other life events. Why not for death? And after you've prepared for death, you'll enjoy each day of life that much more.

APPRECIATION

The following people have helped me by sharing their experiences, advice and suggestions, and by pointing me to other resources: Mary Beth and Bob Adair, Lucy Alexander, Tia Andrews, Sandy and Ron Angle, Joan Randall Bowes, Ann Dickinson, Maggie Elkins, Rosalie Faull, Patricia Gill, Joan Goranson, The Reverend Ronald Greiser, Jr., Margaret Gupta, Henry Hamburger, Sunni Hamilton, Sharon Hartmann, Marianne and Kerry Hines, Margaret Hines, Marty Hines,Bill Holmes, Mary Hooper, John Hundley, Paul Jones, Jeannette Carlberg Kaulfers, Sarah Kerr, Rosa and Howard Leonard, Gerald Liedl, Betsy MacCord, Theodora Mason, Lois Mays, Beje Oliver, Virginia

Pausch, Barbara Parrish, Sarah and Paul Rice, Elizabeth Scott, Sue Sweeney, William Tetzlaff, Gail Thompson, Claudia and Mills Tomlin, Rita and Tommy Vaughan and Robin Willis.

Thanks to Lois Hobart, who suggested the title of this book.

And my special thanks to my daughter Catherine Cantieri, for her editing expertise and for being my strong supporter and helper when Tom died, and to her husband Jason Bowling, for many reasons. May they not need Part II for many years.

HOW TO USE THIS BOOK

I'd recommend that you not read this book in one sitting. Not only is it intended to be a reference work, the subject matter can be, as my editor/daughter put it, "very heavy stuff."

If you and your spouse are still in what I call "The Wonderful Now," start with the first part of the book and work through it at your own pace. You might discover that the conversations you end up having as a result of this book reveal differences between you that could take time to resolve, and the subject matter can be somewhat stressful unto itself, so don't add to the stress by putting yourself on a deadline.

If you've been through the loss of a spouse, skip Part I and go to Part II: "After the Loss." This section will walk you through what to do in the aftermath of your loss, from the first day to the first few years.

Because this book is intended as a how-to, I've included sidebars and symbols to guide you through the text. If you're pressed for time and need to know what to do next, follow these symbols.

 This symbol points to action steps. At the end of each chapter, I've compiled these action steps into a checklist that you can print out or write on, if you wish.

[1] This symbol highlights a recurring action, something that you'll need to re-do or update at least once a year.

📖 This symbol indicates a use for your notebook, and only appears in Part I. I recommend that you start keeping a loose-leaf notebook cataloging all the information you or your survivor will need when one of you passes away.

TABLE OF CONTENTS

It's terrible to discover something unexpected—good or bad—about a loved one after he or she has died. Some devastating examples of secrets revealed. Resolving issues at each stage of marriage.

Caring for yourself and each other: health problems, medications. Types of health insurance you'll need. Emergency care cards and Medic-Alert bracelets and what information should be on each.

Legal documents you may need: power of attorney, trusts, health care directive and health care power of attorney. Why you may need them, what's in each and how they may be activated and revoked. Examples of these documents.

Which papers you need to save, and for how long. Simple filing systems and computer aids to recordkeeping.

Vital lists you and your survivors will need.

How do you want to be remembered? Write your own obituary. Examples of traditional and even humorous obituaries. What to include, what to leave out and why, and where to have it published.

What kind of funeral or memorial service do you want? Put it in writing. Cremation vs. burial. Religious service? Prepaid funerals: pro and con.

Part II: After the Loss

The tasks you'll need to do immediately after your partner has died and whom to notify. What if death has occurred outside a hospital? Organ donation?

Financial, legal and spiritual tasks. Death certificates: when and where you will need them, and how many. Dealing with Social Security.

Ways others can help you that you may not have considered.

Check mortgage, other loans and debts. Insurance or pension benefits. Activating trusts that have been set up. Avoiding identity theft of yourself and the deceased.

Register the will. Qualify as executor. Transfer title to jointly held property, what to cancel, what to keep the deceased's name on.

This is a stressful time, leaving you vulnerable to illnesses and accidents. How to take care of yourself, your family and pets.

How others have dealt with grief. What helps, how you may react, how to tell if you need counseling or other help.

Removing the deceased's name from various places where our life is recorded. How to transfer frequent flyer miles. Thank-you notes: who should be thanked, and why.

The pros and cons of moving to a new home. Suggestions for making the house more "mine" than "ours." Maintaining a household alone.

Your new life—as a single, widowed person. The benefits and dangers of new relationships.

Part I: The Wonderful Now

CHAPTER 1
ARE YOU READY?

It took only a few seconds to change the rest of my life.

The Sunday before Thanksgiving was a lovely sunny day, warm for November. My husband, Tom Cantieri, had rented a van and we were helping our daughter Catherine and her friend Kerrie move into a townhouse. While I organized the kitchen, Tom and the girls left in the rental van to pick up Kerrie's furniture.

I had no way of knowing I had just seen Tom alive for the last time.

I wasn't worried about him, though maybe I should have been. Tom's doctor had given him a checkup in September and said that the steel mitral valve in Tom's heart was performing perfectly. Tom could do whatever he felt like doing, and on that weekend he felt like moving furniture. It's true that he had said he felt out of breath when he went up the steep stairs of the townhouse, so I'd told him the rest of us would carry things upstairs.

He went to the foot of the steps and called up to Catherine and Kerrie that they needed to go for Kerrie's furniture so he'd be able to return the van that evening.

The girls came down and got in the van, and Tom backed

out and started toward the street.

I was lining a cabinet with shelf paper when I heard a thud. Moments later, Kerrie rushed in, out of breath. "Tom has collapsed at the wheel," she said.

I ran out with her to where the van sat wedged against a newspaper box at the edge of the parking lot. Tom was slumped over, limp. Catherine had called 911 and was sobbing, "Keep breathing, Dad." I touched his neck and wrist and thought I could feel a pulse.

I didn't know until much later when I took a first-aid course that I should have laid him flat across the seat of the van and tried CPR. But it probably wouldn't have made a difference. What I didn't detect was the ticking sound of the steel valve in his heart. It had stopped.

It seemed to take forever for the Rescue Squad to arrive. The police followed, as there had been a "traffic accident" when Tom hit the newspaper box. While the medics put an oxygen mask on Tom, and collared his neck to keep him upright, Catherine and I answered questions about the accident and Tom's health. They also checked his Medic Alert bracelet. The traffic cop had his own questions.

After about half an hour, Tom was in the ambulance heading for Riverside Hospital, siren screaming. I rode along, numb with shock. I heard a medic say, "I can't get a carotid," and when Tom was taken from the ambulance, the medics were still doing chest compressions. I sensed that he was dead, and yet I hoped against hope that he was not.

When Catherine and Kerrie arrived at the hospital, we were taken to a small waiting room. After a while, a chaplain came in and said quietly, "Your husband has died." I was too numb to think beyond that moment. He'd been my husband and my best friend for over half my life, and now he was gone forever.

Catherine and I clung together in our grief while the chaplain stood waiting. He didn't attempt to console us, but eventually asked, "What would you like to have done with the body? I have a list of funeral homes."

Tom was now just "the body" and I was a widow. I had joined a vast sisterhood. I felt cheated. He'd only been retired for a year, and we had so many plans for our "golden years" that now would never happen.

"He wanted to be cremated," I said. We had discussed this. I was at least spared choosing a coffin and arranging for burial.

The chaplain said he'd call the Cremation Society, who would see to everything and get in touch with me the next day.

Kerrie went to stay overnight with friends. Catherine and I returned to a quiet house, where a few hours earlier Tom had been laughing, telling a joke and enjoying breakfast.

The real grief, the uncontrollable weeping and the agonizing "if only"s came later. That afternoon and for the next few weeks my mind whirled with all that had to be done, the decisions I had to make. I went through the hours working like a robot.

Besides the usual details I had to take care of—notifying friends and relatives, writing his obituary, planning his funeral service and arranging for all the out-of-towners who'd arrive—I had some tasks that were unique to us, and fairly urgent.

Tom had been teaching an evening class at a local college with two sessions remaining; we'd booked a cruise for 10 days later; he'd been driving a rental van when he collapsed and crashed and he'd made reservations for our Thanksgiving dinner at a hotel. All these had to be dealt with.

Fortunately he'd made out the exam for the class and provided a set of answers. A colleague of his took over the class, graded the exam and submitted the grades. A friend of mine offered to go on the cruise with me, but I knew I wouldn't enjoy it, so I canceled, and filled out insurance refund forms stating the reason: "death of husband."

Catherine arranged for the van to be towed and notified the insurance company. We changed the dinner reservations from three to two, and donated what Tom's dinner would have cost to a charity for the homeless.

That all sounds efficient, but there were glitches. The cremation society was supposed to call, but when they hadn't in 24 hours, I called them. They'd misread the number on the police report and had gotten a message that our phone had been disconnected. I made an appointment and drove aimlessly for an hour looking for the place, lost on the unfamiliar streets. I forgot an important doctor's appointment I'd had as a follow-up to my colonoscopy. I scheduled Tom's funeral for the following Saturday, though it was the Thanksgiving weekend.

In the next few months, I had to register Tom's will and qualify as executor; cancel his insurance policies, memberships, credit cards and appointments; have major repairs made on the house that we'd discussed; transfer car titles; meet with Social Security personnel—and attempt to enjoy Christmas, which had been Tom's birthday.

Almost daily I discovered some new requirement or task I hadn't anticipated, and often was ill equipped for. And it was hard to get used to living alone, without Tom to take care of things or calm me down after some minor fiasco.

Several people offered me advice and help, mostly in handling investments, but Tom had chosen a financial adviser for us, and I trusted him. The manager of rental units we owned out of state assured me he'd continue to "take care of everything" so I wouldn't have to worry. He offered to buy the property for what I thought was a low price.

I didn't feel prepared to handle rental property, and I wanted to sell and simplify my life, but I didn't want to be taken advantage of financially. That property represented a substantial part of our assets.

One day, unexpectedly, a realtor called saying he had buyers looking for condos like ours at the edge of the campus and he said he'd list them at 50 percent more than the manager had offered. I sold. The manager was furious.

The newly widowed are advised to make no big changes during the first year. Selling the property was just such a change, but it was the right move, and it showed me that I could make decisions on my own and need not be "taken care of."

The Sudden Impact of Widowhood

Death can come at any age—suddenly, as in Tom's case, or at the end of a long illness—but it's never easy for the survivor. Nothing I write can take away the pain of grief and loss, but by sharing my experiences and those of other bereaved men and women, I think I can help prepare others for the death of their life's partner, and guide them through the necessary steps that follow.

In the meantime, before that death occurs, you can love and enjoy each other, knowing that whichever of you survives will have an easier widowhood than he or she might have had otherwise. And that's a good gift for the one you love.

Checklist for Couples

Here's a list of questions for each of you. If you answer No to two or more questions, you can benefit from *Til Death Us Do Part*.

☐ Do you have a will that's been prepared or updated within the past three years?

☐ Do you know where it is, and could you locate it quickly?

☐ If you had to evacuate your home in an emergency, would you know what to take?

☐ Could you assemble everything and be ready to leave in half an hour?

☐ Do you know each other's financial information? Do you know where the financial records are kept?

☐ Do you know what your mate wishes to have done in case of extraordinary illness or accident that leaves him/her in a coma or a vegetative state?

☐ Have you put this in writing to protect the other against having to make heartbreaking decisions and possibly facing a lawsuit from other heirs or a charge of murder?

☐ Do you both know how to use all your appliances and electronics and care for your motor vehicles?

☐ Do you know where the guarantees, instructions and service records for those items are?

☐ Have you each given the other a power of attorney and a medical power of attorney?

☐ Do you know what these documents provide?

☐ If your partner died suddenly, would you know what to do legally and whom to call?

☐ Do you have the names, addresses and phone numbers of your partner's closest friends and relatives he/she would want notified of accident, illness or death?

☐ Do you know what you would each want as a funeral?

☐ Have you written your obituary?

☐ Do you have photos, videos or other recordings of each other and of the two of you together in happy times?

One hundred percent of us will die. Less than 10 percent of us are prepared, legally, financially and medically.

Are you?

CHAPTER 2
MANAGING THE BASICS

Marriage is more than a love match. It's a legal contract and a social and financial arrangement, much as a business. Businesses make provisions for the death or departure of one of the partners, and so should you. If you die without a will, your state will see that your assets are distributed in a logical way, though it may not be what you would want. However, the state won't handle the details of your everyday life. That's up to you.

Organizing your life may seem daunting, but the good news is that you can make changes a few at a time, at your own pace. And most of the changes won't cost you a cent.

When you promised to "love, honor and cherish," you probably concentrated on the "love" and gave little thought to balancing checkbooks, changing the oil in the car or getting along with neighbors. And "until death do us part" seemed a long way off.

But imagine for a moment that your spouse has died. Could you go on living in your present home, continuing your present lifestyle? Would you want to? How would you manage?

"I don't know what I'd do if anything happened to John. He handles the money and I never even write checks," Del confided. Her husband laughed. "I don't know where Del keeps things and I'm a total loss in the kitchen. If something happened to her, I'd starve. I might as well go to Jump-Off Rock." But something *will* happen to Del or John, and the other will be left in a quandary. What about you?

Starting now, you can do two major things to avoid problems for your survivor:

Become versatile. Trade "his" and "hers" tasks. Learn how to use your household appliances, cook a day's worth of meals, make simple household repairs and handle your money.

Get to know your doctors, dentists, garage mechanics, spiritual advisors, bank employees, vet and groomer if you have pets and your neighbors.

Your Notebook

In a loose-leaf notebook, begin a simple instruction manual for now and later. Not only will this notebook be invaluable when one of you passes away, it can also be a lifesaver in the event of evacuation, hospitalization for one or both of you or any other event where you or someone else will have to operate or recreate your household.

> On the first page of your notebook, write the names, addresses, phone numbers and email addresses of your nearest neighbors.

Know Your Neighbors

> Give a door key to one or more neighbors. Indicate this in your notebook, and let the neighbors know that you'll be willing to look after things for them in return.

> Give your neighbors the names and phone numbers

of your close relatives and ask permission to share their contact information with your family members.

Learn Automotive Care

Sue took an automotive repair class and a handyman class at the local community college. "It was money well spent," she said. "Now, I get more respect and better service from repairmen, and a lot I can take care of myself." Could you? Do you know how to check the fluids and tire pressure of your car?

- If you don't know how to perform automotive maintenance, take your car to the dealer or a mechanic on a less busy day, or ask a knowledgeable neighbor to show you.

- [1] If you live in a state that requires auto inspection, make sure you know when your inspection is due. A widowed neighbor, Madge, confessed that she'd gotten a threatening letter from the Department of Motor Vehicles when her inspection wasn't done by the required date. Her husband had taken care of the car and she never knew it had to be inspected.

- For your safety and peace of mind, join an automobile club, such as AAA. Engines can stop running (usually on a rainy day at a busy intersection!), tires can blow or be punctured (usually on a dark night) and strange things can go wrong with your car just when you need it most. Keep the membership card in your wallet, with a photocopy in the glove compartment of the car, along with the inspection certificate, insurance card and photocopy of your registration card. The original should be in your auto file. And buy and learn to use a GPS. I didn't have one until my friend Jo gave me a GPS—after I got lost twice trying to get through Raleigh.

In your notebook, head up a separate page for each car you own with the make of the car, such as "04 Ford Mustang." Then write the name, address and phone number of a garage you trust, the vehicle identification number of the car, the suggested tire pressure and type and amount of oil and other fluids it requires. Some of this is in the owner's manual, but a lot of it isn't. Besides, you don't want to be constantly reading the owner's manual for simple information.

Keep and file the service records for your car. They're important if a problem recurs or there is a manufacturer's recall. (I describe filing in more detail in Chapter 10, "Keeping Tabs.")

Get to Know Your House

Learn to operate all the appliances and equipment in your house—including the garage. Do you know where the instructions to your appliances are? Do you know how to change the filters for your furnace and air conditioner, and what size filters to buy? Renters of a house we owned burned out the compressor on an air conditioner by not changing its filters even though we had furnished a box of them.

Drains may need an occasional flushing with drain cleaner. After Tom's death I neglected drain cleaning until the washing machine pipe overflowed. I had to summon Roto-Rooter, who came at 10:30 at night. I learned an expensive lesson. Drain cleaning was something Tom had taken care of, but the task was now mine.

Do you know where the circuit box is? Are the switches clearly labeled so you'd know what to turn off before making repairs? Electrocution is a hard lesson.

Do you know how to reset the circuit breaker? A friend called an electrician when the power went off in her kitchen. He flicked a switch in the circuit box and charged his usual fee for a house call. Another expensive lesson.

> Make a file for each appliance or piece of electronic equipment you own. Each file should its include date of purchase, guarantees or warranties, instructions for use, parts list and the name and phone number of someone to call for repairs.

Our files on appliances came in handy when the dishwasher quit working on Christmas Eve. I knew whom to call for repairs, but when I saw the date we'd purchased the dishwasher, I decided to buy a new one.

Pets

> If you have pets, start a file for each one, with records of vets visits, illnesses and shots, along with receipts for licensing the pet, since the tags on your pet's collar can get lost. And because pets themselves can get lost, keep a current photo of your pet on hand as well.

Finances

Tom and I divided household tasks when we both had outside jobs. He did most of the laundry and vacuuming and looked after the cars, while I cooked, dusted and cleaned bathrooms. We took turns paying bills. However, when he retired, he took over handling our finances, and changed a lot of procedures. After he died, I had to get help from our bank manager to straighten out the checkbook because of automatic payments and online banking Tom had arranged that I knew nothing about.

He'd also looked after the finances of rental property we owned. The manager called a month after Tom's death to say that real estate taxes were past due. According to the checkbook, Tom had written a check but it had not cleared. I wired money to the tax collector. Later I found the envelope, stamped and addressed, with the tax bill and check, attached to a wall calendar, ready to be mailed on the appropriate date. I hadn't thought to look there.

[1] To keep track of bills, make a list in your notebook of those that regularly recur. Name the company, the date the bill is likely to arrive and the date it's due. Consider having regular payments, such as for utilities, taken directly from your checking account. This comes in handy not just in the event of illness or death, but when you want to be away on vacation. Note these payments in your checkbook.

When Tom and I bought our first house, we just paid bills as they arrived, and it was about six months before we decided to work out a budget. "How much are we paying for electricity?" he asked.

I searched the checkbook and receipts. Nothing. We hadn't been billed for electricity the whole time we'd lived in our new house. We called the electric company to report this and ask for a bill. One arrived two days later, marked 'Final Notice', with a warning that if we didn't pay within three days, our electricity would be shut off! With a bill-paying system in place from the first, this error would have been picked up much sooner. We were about to leave for the beach, but detoured by the utility company's office to pay our bill.

Learn Skills

 Print or photocopy this checklist and staple it into your notebook, checking off tasks you know how to do or as you accomplish them. (If you own this book, you can just write directly in it.) If they don't apply to you—for example, if you don't own a car— cross those items off your list. Try to learn one new skill each week.

Skills Checklist

	Husband	Wife
Know your 3 nearest neighbors		
Check tire pressure and add air to tires		
Check oil, radiator fluid and battery fluid		
Check car inspection and registration dates		
Join AAA		
Have a GPS and know how to use it		
Know what the various switches in the circuit box control and how to reset them		
Know how to change furnace filters		
Use dishwasher		
Use vacuum cleaner and know how to empty it and/or change disposable bags		
Use clothes washer and pre-treat stains		
Use dryer and clean lint filter		
Know how to prepare 3 food items		
Can follow a recipe for new entrees		
Know how to shut off the water to your house		
Know the names and phone numbers of household contractors, such as carpet cleaners		
Know how to change the answering machine message		
Know how to use and recharge cell phone		
Know how to reset electronic clocks		
Know how to check and reset smoke alarms		
Can write checks and balance checkbook		
Know when your regular bills fall due		
Know at least one teller at your bank, and go there often enough so that you are recognized		

Checklist for Chapter 2

- ☐ Begin keeping a notebook for the operations of your household.

- ☐ On the first page of your notebook, write the names, addresses, phone numbers and email addresses of your nearest neighbors.

- ☐ Give a door key to one or more neighbors. Indicate this in your notebook, and let the neighbors know that you'll be willing to look after things for them in return.

- ☐ Give your neighbors the names and phone numbers of your close relatives and ask permission to share their contact information with your family members.

- ☐ If you don't know how to perform automotive maintenance, take your car to the dealer or a mechanic on a less busy day, or ask a knowledgeable neighbor to show you.

- ☐ If you live in a state that requires auto inspection, make sure you know when your inspection is due.

- ☐ In your notebook, write the following for every car you own: its year, make and model; the name, address and phone number of a garage you trust; its vehicle identification number; its suggested tire pressure and type and the amount of oil and other fluids it requires.

- ☐ Keep and file the service records for your car.

- ☐ Learn to operate all the appliances and equipment in your house—including the garage.

- ☐ Make a file for each appliance or piece of electronic equipment you own.

- ☐ If you have pets, start a file for each one, with records of vets visits, illnesses and shots, along with receipts for licensing.

- ☐ Make a list in your notebook of regularly recurring bills.

- ☐ Learn how to perform all skills in the Skills Checklist.

CHAPTER 3
WHAT ARE YOU WORTH?

Scientists say that the minerals that make up our bodies are worth only a few dollars. As individuals, we are priceless to those who love us. But how rich are you in worldly assets? Maybe more than you think. Or, depending on what the stock market and real estate market are doing right now, maybe not. Whichever way your fortune is moving, before you make a will, you need to assess your net worth.

Checking your net worth is also essential to making present-day spending decisions and to acquainting each of you with what he or she can expect as the survivor. An all-too-common plaint after a spouse's death is, "I had no idea…" Undisclosed debts can show up to wreck your plans, or hidden and unknown assets can go unclaimed.

Assets

If you own your own home, it's probably your biggest asset. Other assets might include stocks and bonds, rental property, insurance policies, pensions and IRAs, bank accounts, loans made to others that you reasonably expect to collect, expected Social Security benefits, coin or stamp collections, antiques, art work, automobiles, jewelry and home furnishings.

Create a section in your notebook called "Net Worth." To start figuring your net worth as a couple, put several sheets of paper in this section and start listing your assets under the following categories. Each category of asset should have its own sheet.

Real Estate

Check your latest real estate tax bill for the approximate value of your residence. However, if your property is appraised for tax purposes at a fraction of the true value, or is assessed only irregularly or when a sale occurs, you can check the local real estate ads for homes listed similar to yours.

Be as realistic and accurate as you can; don't list what you expect your property to be worth someday. Assume for this exercise that you had to sell your home immediately.

 If you own your residence outright, write down the value, along with a brief description of the property.

For example, "Two-story brick single-family residence at 102 Maple Street, Hometown, MS. 2,400 square feet, 4 bedrooms, 2 baths, built 1989. Attached garage, quarter-acre lot."

 If you have a mortgage, create another sheet for your net worth titled "Liabilities" and list the amount of your mortgage there.

 If you own rental property, write down the address, type of property (as "townhouse," "single-family dwelling," etc.), a description, date of purchase and the value for each separate property.

 Create a separate sheet titled Income, and list the monthly or yearly net income from that property.

Stocks and Bonds

 List all the stocks and bonds you own. Include the name of the stock, how many shares you own, date of purchase and approximate value, according to your latest brokerage statement. Update this list periodically, as you buy/sell securities. The easiest way is to attach a copy of the statement your broker sends. If you trade online, print out a current statement of your balances and stocks owned.

Insurance Policies

 List the value of any paid-up life insurance policies, with company name, policy number, date issued, terms, beneficiary, person to notify and his or her phone number. If you are a veteran, you may have a government life insurance policy. You may also have easily-overlooked life insurance as part of a mortgage or as a condition of employer-covered health insurance.

Only paid-up life insurance policies can be counted as part of your net worth, but all kinds of insurance will be valuable to your survivors.

 Create another sheet labeled Insurance and list all of your policies here.

For example, you may have accidental death and dismemberment insurance through your automobile association or bought as a separate policy. This will pay off if you die in an accident. Special types of insurance, such as cancer or intensive care policies, will be valuable if your death is preceded by a lengthy or expensive hospitalization, but these policies are not counted as part of your net worth now.

Term insurance has value only as long as you continue paying premiums. You can't borrow funds using it as collateral, nor can you cash it in early.

I have a small $10,000 term life insurance policy as part of my Virginia Retirement System pension, and a travel insurance policy that would pay my heirs if I were killed while traveling. These will be part of my estate, but can't be counted as assets.

Also list your health, long term care, fire and flood policies on your residence and any liability or special insurance you have. These also are very important, but have no intrinsic value as part of your net worth. They are for the financial protection of you and your loved ones, and come into play only after an unfortunate incident.

All insurance policies should be in your safe deposit box or in your 'grab-and-go' box, clearly marked so your survivor can find them quickly.

Bank Accounts

List all bank accounts, which bank each account is in, how each is owned (the names listed on the account), the account number and the rate of interest.

Give the approximate amount as of a certain date, and update it quarterly or when bank statements arrive.

Note: Get to know the people at your local bank. After a death occurs, you will repeatedly need the services of a notary, and banks all have personnel who are notaries. Inquire about the best rates for your savings.

Pensions, Annuities and Other Retirement Income

How much income do you each expect from Social Security? You can request a report yearly. List the figures on your Income sheet, along with each social security number.

If you can expect a pension, list the amount, the date on which it begins and what the source is. Does it continue after the death of the main pensioner? In what amount? Do you have an IRA? How much will you be required to take out per year after your retirement? Do you plan to begin withdrawing money at the earliest possible age or not until the mandatory withdrawal age (70½)? What bank or financial institution has your IRA?

Do you have an annuity? What does/will it pay yearly? Can it be inherited by your survivor or does it cease at your death? Is it guaranteed to pay for a set number of years?

An annuity and an IRA are definite assets. Social Security payments are not assets as such, inasmuch as they can't be 'cashed in' but they may be extremely important to your survivor. Pensions should be counted as assets if they can be taken in a lump sum or if they are guaranteed for a set number of years.

Automobiles

Check the automotive "blue book" for the value of your vehicle, or read local ads for autos similar to yours. Give a brief description of your car or cars, such as "Ford Taurus station wagon, 2001." If you own it outright, list its value on your Asset sheet, being aware that motor vehicles begin to depreciate the moment you drive them off the dealer's lot.

If you have a loan against the car, list the amount still owed on the Liability sheet.

Loans

 If you have loaned money to anyone, list the amount owed you, the rate of interest, the debtor's name, address and phone number and the date payments are due.

Keep a copy of the signed loan note a file in your home labeled something like "Guarantees and Important Receipts." The note itself should be in your safe deposit box or "grab-and-go" box. Note payments made on your Assets list, and subtract the amounts from the principal owed.

If you have outstanding balances on your credit cards or have other unsecured loans such as student loans, list them on the Liability sheet, and note interest rates and date payments are due.

Miscellaneous Property

If you have valuable jewelry (such as diamond rings), antique furniture, artwork or collections, have them appraised and insured. Coin or stamp collections may be kept in your safe deposit box.

 These items, along with china and silverware, should be included in your net worth estimate.

You can get an idea of their value by browsing at antique shops or pawn shops. If you purchased these items, list the date of purchase and purchase price. You may also have inherited family items. If so, list the age of the item, the date you acquired it, and its value.

Many homeowners insurance companies estimate, as part of their coverage, that furnishings are worth about half the value of the dwelling. For instance, if your home is insured for $200,000, replacement value of your furnishings would be $100,000. However, real estate has escalated in value more than furniture has. Only you can determine if the insurance estimates are accurate for your particular home and furnishings. If you have musical instruments, such as a grand piano, allow extra for them.

 Make an inventory of your home's items.

The law firm of Oast and Hook in Portsmouth, Virginia, advises its clients to inventory household items, both as an indication of net worth and in case there is a question of value for insurance coverage or to file a claim with the Federal Emergency Management Agency (FEMA).

They recommend Quicken Home Inventory Manager software, which enables you to inventory each room, then drag and drop photos of the various items into your inventory. Back this up on a flash drive, and print a paper copy as well. If you're not computer-literate, go from room to room with your notebook, itemizing and photographing the contents.

Miscellaneous Assets

 Have you written a book or patented an invention on which royalties may be due you or your heirs? List the name of the item, the company that may be paying and an estimate of amount you expect.

If you are a partner in a business or own a business, share the details with your spouse.

Listing your assets and liabilities for a business or rental property may be complicated enough that you would require the services of an accountant and a lawyer. These professionals should have been involved in setting up the company or purchasing the income-producing property, but if you have been operating informally, it's not too late to seek professional help. Don't leave a mess for your grieving survivor to handle.

Liabilities

If you have a mortgage, a car loan or credit card bills, or owe any money to any other people or institutions, these are liabilities, and should listed on your Liabilities sheet.

Your net worth can now be determined by subtracting the value of your total liabilities from the value of your total assets. This number might be a surprise to you, pleasant or otherwise.

Your Net Worth Statement

When you've assessed your financial situation, you can see if you're financially prepared for the future. If not, what changes need to be made? Should you cash out your paid-up insurance, bank the proceeds in a "rainy day" account and buy term insurance? It's important to have at least six months' expenses in accessible funds, but depending on your age and health, you may not be able to buy term insurance. Do you need to cut down on expenses and pay off credit cards? How soon can you pay off your mortgage?

 Recalculate your net worth every year or so. As you pay down your liabilities, or take on new loans or debts, your net worth can change. It can also change as your assets appreciate or you acquire new ones. Hopefully, you can watch your net worth grow every year and this exercise can become a point of pride.

Sample Net Worth Statement

Assets

Residence: 2-story brick house, built 1989, on .25 acre lot at 210 Oak Street, Anytown, OH	$257,000
Rental Property: 1 bedroom condo, built 2005, 132 Water Drive, Beachfront, NC	138,000
Total value of stocks and bonds held in account at American Funds	114,385
Certificate of Deposit, 1.5 percent interest, due 9/10/2012, First National Bank, Anytown, OH	10,000
Paid up life insurance, Acme, Policy # 123456789	75,000
Savings Account, First National Bank, 1% interest, #9876543	6,872
IRA, present values; Jane's, $52,000; Joe's $70,000	122,000
04 Ford Mustang Convertible	7,800
2 diamond rings, appraised by Goldcrafters, Inc.	6,500
Household furnishings and art (inventory attached)	61,750
Total Assets	**$799,307**

Liabilities

Mortgage on residence	$132,923
Mortgage on rental property	59,645
Student loan for graduate school	49, 802
Amount owed on Visa, Master Card and American Express	4,441
Total Liabilities	**$246,811**
Net Worth for Joan & Joe	**$552,496**

Your own net worth categories will vary.

Checklist for Chapter 3

☐ Create a section in your notebook called "Net Worth."

☐ List every asset you own by its category, with a separate sheet for each category: Real Estate, Stocks and Bonds, Insurance, Bank Accounts, Automobiles, Loans and Miscellaneous Property.

☐ List all of the amounts you owe others on a separate sheet, called Liabilities.

☐ List all of the monthly or annual income you expect to receive, including income from rental properties and retirement income, on a sheet labeled Income.

☐ Subtract your total Liabilities from your total Assets to determine your Net Worth.

☐ Repeat this exercise every year to reflect how your assets and liabilities change.

CHAPTER 4
WHAT'S IN THE BOX?

To protect yourself and your property, you'll need three special boxes: a bank safe deposit box for valuables, a "grab-and-go" box for emergencies and a box or large file of past tax records. These are in addition to your regular household files, which will be described in Chapter 10, "Keeping Tabs."

Some couples also rent public storage units away from their home to keep seldom-used items and business and financial records for longer than the recommended time. Just remember to pay the bill on the storage unit when it's due, or your belongings may be sold and your records hauled off to the dump where they may be destroyed or pillaged for valuable data by identity thieves.

Whether you keep a little or a lot, it's important to remember where it is and for you and your survivors to be able to locate it when it's needed or wanted. Safety and security are concerns, too. What if you opened one of your storage boxes to discover that rats or silverfish had eaten your documents, or that moisture and mildew had rendered everything unreadable?

Choose carefully where you store your documents and other valuables, and make sure you and your survivors can access them.

Safe Deposit Box

 Rent a safe deposit box in a bank that's convenient to where you live; make sure it's large enough to hold valuable items that you don't need on a regular basis.

What goes in a safe deposit box?

☐　A copy of your wills, not the originals. (Your box may be legally sealed at your death, just when your will is needed.)

☐　Jewelry that you wear only on special occasions

☐　Bonds: US Savings Bonds as well as corporate bonds, and stock certificates for stocks not held by your broker

☐　Gold, coin collections and stamp collections

☐　Promissory notes, deeds and other valuable legal documents

☐　Patents and copyrights

☐　Titles to motor vehicles and boats: You will only need these if you are selling or otherwise transferring titles.

☐　An inventory and photos of home furnishings, especially antiques. Duplicates, or a flash drive containing these records, should go in your "grab-and-go" box.

☐　Birth certificates, marriage licenses, divorce decrees, military discharge papers, social security cards, and passports. These, or scanned copies, may be kept in the "grab-and-go" box.

The rent on a safe deposit box is payable by the year and can be deducted from your bank account. It may also be a tax-deductible expense, depending on what you store in the safe deposit box.

You will be given a key to the box, sometimes two keys, and will have to sign a signature card. You may also be asked to provide a password.

 If you do need a password, chose something both of you can remember, and record it in your list of passwords (see Chapter 11, "Making a List").

When you need to open your safe deposit box, you may be asked to provide your password, and you will have to sign a register. You'll be accompanied into the vault by a bank employee, who will unlock one of the locks on the box. You must then unlock the other. After you have used the box, you'll return it to its space, lock it, sign out and inform the bank employee that you are finished.

Make an inventory of the safe deposit box contents, put one copy in the box itself and keep the other at home in a special file or in your "grab-and-go" box.

Both of you should know where the keys are kept. They will probably come in a small, sturdy envelope. It's a good idea to have a trustworthy third person know the whereabouts of your safe deposit box and keys, in case of an accident that involves both of you. That person's name and signature should be on file at the bank where the safe deposit box is located.

Go to the bank and open your safe deposit box at least yearly, preferably every six months. Check to make sure that what you have inventoried is actually there. If you take anything out of the box, cross through that item on your inventory, note "Removed," write the date and initial beside the notation.

If a death is expected, **go to the bank and remove everything from the safe deposit box**. Once a death occurs, the funeral home or cremation society will notify Social Security, who will notify your bank.

The box may be sealed by the bank after a death until an administrator of your estate has qualified with the court. You would thus be unable to get legal documents and other items at the very time you need them most.

My husband's cousin Josephine was widowed very young. As she said, "I was naïve, and because of that, I nearly starved. For a year, everything was tied up and the safe deposit box was sealed. I couldn't touch any of my late husband's property. I couldn't so much as buy myself a lipstick without getting permission from a lawyer."

She remarried, and many years later, when she awoke to find her second husband dead in bed beside her, she remembered the safe deposit box incident. "I didn't tell anyone he was dead. I got dressed in one of my newest, prettiest outfits, put on make-up and a big smile and cleaned out the box. I chatted with the bank tellers about the vacation we were planning, and withdrew most of our savings as well. Only then did I go home and call the authorities to report his death."

"Grab-and-Go" Box

If you were told to evacuate your home, as thousands of people have had to do within the past few years ahead of hurricanes, forest fires and other emergencies, how long would it take you to gather your important papers?

You wouldn't want to spend a lot of time searching for something when you should be gathering the family, pets and supplies, and preparing to leave. Instead, plan ahead.

 Get together all the papers that you might find difficult, expensive or time-consuming to replace, and put them in a single box, about the size of a shoe box. If you're computer-savvy, scan them, save them to a flash drive and store it in a safe place, such as your safe deposit box. Make printed copies of all important documents.

The "grab-and-go" box need not be an actual box, but only a sturdy cardboard ("leatherette") folder with elastic closing, such as banks and realtors use. They are readily available from office supply stores. Or you may prefer a decorated box that can be prominently placed for easy 'grabbing' and which would be an attractive element in your room's décor.

After the evacuation, you might return to find your home destroyed or severely damaged. You'd need to prove what you owned for insurance purposes. This is where the contents of your "grab-and-go" box come in.

What Goes in a "Grab-and-Go" Box?

- ☐ Originals of wills unless these are kept at your lawyer's office, or are stored electronically in a document bank
- ☐ Living wills: instructions for your final days
- ☐ Bank account numbers, name of the bank(s) and phone number(s)
- ☐ Credit card numbers and 800- numbers to call if the cards are lost or stolen. The easiest way to do this is to photocopy the front and back of your credit cards.
- ☐ Copies of prescriptions for medicines and eyeglasses
- ☐ Vaccination certificates for the family and pets
- ☐ A set of house keys, keys to your file cabinet/desk and the key to your safe deposit box
- ☐ List of the contents of your safe deposit box
- ☐ Insurance policy numbers, company name and phone number
- ☐ Copy of the inventory of your home's contents

☐ Name and phone number of someone to notify in case of emergency. This should be on the very top of the contents of your box.

Tax Record Box

You never know when you'll be audited. I was audited in 2006 for 2004 taxes. Even with good records, it was a stressful experience, but without those records, I might have had to spend many days trying to piece together sales receipts, brokerage receipts, etc. and might have ended up paying taxes I didn't owe.

⚡ Designate a box to hold your tax records. This box should be large enough to hold at least three—and even up to seven—years' worth of complete tax records.

⚡ In your tax box, keep a copy of the entire 1040 form and any other supplemental forms you signed, as well as copies of W-2 forms showing employment income, and backup materials. For example, if you had income from rental property, you'll need to keep copies of repair bills, purchases made, depreciation schedules and amount of rent charged.

⚡ 1 If you operate a business from your home in addition to your regular job, keep a record of miles driven on business, supplies, license costs, etc.

If you have a room set aside for your business, you can deduct a portion of your rent or mortgage payment, a portion of your phone/internet bill and a portion of your utility bills. Note, however, that this will be scrutinized more than most other deductions, as the deduction has been so often misused. You may need an accountant to make sure your records are accurate. His/

her fee will be tax deductible.

 1 Keep a record of where your money goes. Few banks return canceled checks, but your bank statements probably show miniature facsimiles. Your credit card bills showing charitable contributions, medical expenses, and other deductible items should also be kept, along with letters thanking you for your contributions. These letters are probably the most important proof you will need to substantiate your claimed deductions.

Many professionals say it's only necessary to keep three years' records, but if you have the space, I'd go for seven.

Self-Storage Units

As we accumulate more "stuff," we outgrow our available space, so many of us rent metal storage units away from home. If you rent such a unit, choose a secure, well-lighted location that is not flood prone.

 Write in your household notebook the exact address, driving directions, the number of your unit and the office phone number of the manager.

Make an inventory of everything you're storing in the unit, and take photos of the items. Keep the photos, the list, the key to the unit and the name, location and unit number in your "grab-and-go" box.

In an emergency or in the shock of a death, it's easy to forget the things that are stored and not often seen. Nearly every dry cleaner has clothing brought in that was never reclaimed and paid for, and nearly every owner of storage lockers has padlocked units full of someone's property—perhaps valuable, perhaps not, but forgotten. If you don't pay the rent or remove your belongings, the lock will be cut and your items auctioned. Several cable networks have even created shows about what happens to these items—and it's not pretty.

During warm weather, my local dry cleaner stores all winter clothing that's been brought in for cleaning. I took advantage of the offer, happy to free up closet space. And to make sure my clothing—including my favorite coat—didn't get lost, I photocopied the receipt and sent it to my daughter, along with instructions for claiming the items in case of my death before next winter.

With care and good records, your belongings won't be among the lost.

Checklist for Chapter 4

☐ Rent a safe deposit box in a bank that's convenient to where you live; make sure it's large enough to hold valuable items that you don't need on a regular basis.

☐ If you need a password for your safe deposit box, chose something both of you can remember, and record it in your list of passwords.

☐ Make an inventory of the safe deposit box contents, put one copy in the box itself and keep the other at home in a special file or in your "grab-and-go" box.

☐ Go to the bank and open your safe deposit box at least yearly, preferably every six months.

☐ If a death is expected, *go to the bank and remove everything from the safe deposit box.*

☐ Get together all the papers that might be difficult, expensive or time-consuming to replace, and put them in a single box, about the size of a shoe box. This is your "grab-and-go" box.

☐ Designate a box to hold your tax records. This box should be large enough to hold at least three—and even up to seven—years' worth of complete tax records.

☐ In your tax box, keep a copy of the entire 1040 form and any other supplemental forms you signed, as well as copies of W-2 forms showing employment income, and backup materials.

☐ If you operate a business from your home in addition to your regular job, keep a record of miles driven on business, supplies, license costs, etc.

☐ Keep a record of where your money goes. Your credit card bills showing charitable contributions, medical expenses, and other deductible items should also be kept, along with letters thanking you for your contributions.

☐ If you get a self-storage unit, write in your household notebook the exact address, driving directions, the number of your unit and the office phone number of the manager.

CHAPTER 5
MAKING MEMORIES
AND BEING YOURSELF

Shakespeare wrote, "The evil that men do lives after them, the good is oft interred with their bones." What about you? Will you be remembered by your good, or will your survivors have bad thoughts about you? And if you're the survivor, will you have regrets about what you and your mate might have done or said? Will you wish you'd said "I love you" more often, and had more fun together?

If you were suddenly widowed, what memories would you treasure of your mate? If you can't immediately think of a host of good ones, it's time to begin making some.

When Barbara's husband was diagnosed with terminal cancer, they decided to have "an adventure a day." At first they traveled to exotic places they'd talked of for years. As his disease progressed, their "adventures" became simpler, shorter and closer to home—sometimes only a short walk around a nearby lake, or renting an old movie and enjoying a laugh together.

Now that he is gone, Barbara looks back fondly on those final months. Her memories are precious. What kind of memories would you treasure?

Make Memories Now

Building good memories together strengthens and enriches your relationship at any stage, so begin making memories now. Waiting until your spouse is near death may be too late.

> Don't put off taking that trip you've dreamed about. Call up a travel agent and arrange it, or go online and find the best deal you can to your favorite destination.

But your adventures don't have to take you far away. Many small "adventures" are available right where you live and cost little or nothing, but can still create the kind of memories that will sustain you in dark times.

Some memories are unplanned and can't be repeated; they just happen. Two that I look back on with pleasure are quite different. Soon after we moved into a mountainside home, my cat Max jumped up onto a brick ledge along the side of the house and ran to the end. He began at ground level, but at the rear of the house he was 20 feet up. He looked down, realized it was too high to jump and too narrow to turn around. Instead of panicking, he carefully backed the entire way, over 40 feet, while we watched and laughed.

Another time, in church on the Sunday after Easter, the choir had been given the day off and the organist began playing during the Communion service. We'd always enjoyed his excellent playing and expected some musical anthem, not the glorious surprise that came: he sang the anthem in a beautiful, powerful tenor voice, while playing the organ with hands and feet, controlling all the stops and turning his own pages. Truly a magnificent memory.

Wherever you live, there's probably something beautiful to see, something interesting to do. Go out and find it, and enjoy it together: a park bench in a secluded spot; a winter sunrise that paints the sky rose, yellow, lavender and turquoise; a snowfall or drifting colored leaves or a plot of your own flowers.

Do Things Together

 Do something that your partner enjoys that you might not.

Paul never liked gambling, but his wife did. He arranged a trip to Las Vegas, rented an electric scooter so she could move around independently, and stood back to watch her enjoy herself in all the ways gamblers partake of Las Vegas. On a later trip to Hawaii, they also rented an electric scooter so they could explore the beach, stopping off to have lunch or drinks at some beautiful spot overlooking Diamond Head. A few weeks after this trip, she died.

 Take a walk, be it a stroll or a strenuous hike, whenever your schedule allows, and whatever the circumstances.

Barbara and her husband took walks to the very last, though it meant she had to help him into a wheelchair and push it slowly along a paved pathway. Whenever she stopped to rest, they'd look around for something that was different from the previous walk: ducks on a pond, a bird building its nest, tiny wildflowers peeping up through the earth.

Every time of day has something beautiful to enjoy. If your neighborhood is safe, walking at night can be very pleasant, especially in summer when the air cools, lightning bugs flit about and the moon and stars fill the sky above you. Go out and look at meteor showers, eclipses and rainbows. Get out the binoculars and identify the planets and the craters of the moon.

Have a picnic.

It doesn't have to be anything elaborate. You've got to eat anyway, so make it fun, and easy. Remember, this is about creating good memories, not working. We used to pick up fried okra and chili cheesedogs from the supermarket deli and have a picnic on our screened back porch. Now when I'm shopping and see okra and cheesedogs on the steam table, it brings back pleasant memories. For your picnic, go by a deli or the drive-in window of a fast food place for the "fixings" and find a beautiful spot to dine, even if it's your own back porch.

Another of my good memories was having wine and sandwiches by candlelight on our porch one cool spring evening after we'd worked in the garden all day. We showered and dressed, and I spread a tablecloth on a card table, set up by a cozy fire. I'd like to be back there for another evening, but I can only return in memory.

  On the upscale side, treat yourselves sometimes to an elegant, special dinner.

After all, if you were dating, you'd occasionally go out for an expensive evening. Tom and I often recalled a wonderful seafood lunch we'd enjoyed overlooking the harbor of Capri in Italy. We could also laugh about the bad dining decisions we'd sometimes made, and the truly awful meals that resulted.

Put on some music and dance together.

Even better, take dancing lessons so you both know the same steps. Dancing is good for you physically, and it may lead to further intimacy in your relationship. That can create some good memories as well.

Attend each other's reunions.

In the year that Tom died we went to four reunions, almost

as if he knew each would be his last. The most nostalgic was a performance of the Virginia Gentlemen, a singing group of which Tom had been one of the founding members. Another founding member put together a CD of the group singing, with cover photos of the Gentlemen then and now, a priceless memento of that reunion and of his singing.

 Look at each other's school yearbooks and share the memories the various pictures bring back.

You'll get to know each other better and will realize how important memories are. One of my regrets is that Tom and I never did this. I only looked at his high school yearbook after he was dead, and learned things about his youth that I wish I'd known sooner.

Record Your Lives

 Record each other's voices and the voices of your children.

As time passes, your memory of just how your beloved sounded will fade. It can be singing or just talking. Some people preserve the late spouse's voice on the answering machine, saying "You have reached…" It's better than nothing, but you can do better. While there is still time, record something more meaningful.

 If either of you or a family member appears in performances, tape it, if it is permitted. If it's being professionally recorded, buy a copy of the CD.

 Take lots of photos, and label them with names, dates, locations and events.

Take photos not just of special events, but of everyday happenings: cooking, mowing the lawn, assembling some item that came in parts, reading a bedtime story to a child, washing the dog, etc. One of my favorites is of Tom and Catherine cutting a pumpkin into a jack o'lantern, and another is of the two of them bundled up warmly, snow shovels in hand. Don't just save your photos on your computer, where they might be accidentally deleted, but print and put the best in albums, chronologically arranged.

 Go back and look together at photos of special events, such as your wedding, graduations, births of children, etc. and relive the memories of those occasions.

Scan the best old ones into a flash drive or CD for your "grab-and-go" box (see Chapter 4). If you don't have a scanner, you can rent one or you can have a commercial photo lab make a CD of prints.

Even ordinary tasks can turn into a memorable occasion. When Renee and her husband were preparing to move from a large home into a retirement condo, they faced sorting and packing a lifetime's collection of books. Some were to be donated to an archeological society, some given to friends, some moved to the new place. As they went through the books, they chatted about the archeological dig represented in one book, the trip to Budapest when they'd bought this one, the friend who gave that one. "It brought up some wonderful memories," she said, "and some tearful ones too. Then later, after he died, my job was easier because we'd already decided what to do with the books."

Share Your Love Now

 Give each other small gifts that show you know the other's tastes and likes/dislikes.

Write notes and tell each other often how much you love and appreciate him/her. I treasure a card my daughter made at age seven and a handmade valentine from Tom more than an expensive ring he gave me. And I'll always be glad that I told him on a Friday night how important his help and encouragement had been to me in my writing and that I couldn't have done it without him. Two days later he died suddenly.

Start making your memories now. You never know when it may be too late to say or do all the things you've been planning. How much better it is for your spouse to hear fine, loving words, than to have others hear them read at a memorial service.

Celebrate Your Individuality

Of course, while you're making memories together, you still need to continue with things that are important to you as individuals.

You need occasional breaks from each other and need to continue being a person, not just half a couple.

Marty Hines, an estates and trust paralegal and a widow, said, "It's important to maintain friends and interests outside the 'couple.' Among the widows I have worked with, those who didn't maintain their own individuality had periods of depression, were unable to cope with their new single status, and were often an emotional burden on their children."

During their 41 years of marriage, Marty and her husband Anthony had the care of seven children, but managed "time-outs" for each other. He'd look after the children so she could follow her creative interests and spend time with friends, relieving some of the stress of parenthood. She in turn would take over the home duties so he could go fishing or attend football games.

When one of their daughters was getting married, the mistress of ceremonies told the couple to extinguish their individual candles and light a unity candle, signifying that their individual lives were over, and from that point forward they would exist as a couple. "I immediately objected and said that was not true," Marty related. "You should never give up your separate interests, just pare them back a little."

Later, after Anthony died, their children feted Marty on Mother's Day, and told her how much they admired her for carrying on so well alone. "You were strong for us when we were all missing Dad," one said.

Marty's outlook is much like that of Doris. When we were discussing how we would react to a spouse's death, she said, "I was me before I met Rufus and before we married and had the boys. If something happened to them, I'd still be me, and I'd find a way to carry on."

Checklist for Chapter 5

☐ Start planning and going on adventures together, whether it's your "dream vacation" or a nearby adventure that doesn't cost anything.

☐ Do something that your partner enjoys that you might not.

☐ Take a walk together, whenever your schedule allows and whatever the circumstances.

☐ Have a picnic.

☐ From time to time, treat yourselves to an elegant, special dinner.

☐ Put on some music and dance together.

☐ Attend each other's reunions.

☐ Look at each other's school yearbooks and share the memories the various pictures bring back.

☐ Record each other's voices and the voices of your children.

☐ If either of you or a family member appears in performances, tape it, if it is permitted.

☐ Take lots of photos, and label them with names, dates, locations and events.

☐ Go back and look together at photos of special events, such as your wedding, graduations, births of children, etc. and relive the memories of those occasions.

☐ Give each other small gifts that show you know the other's tastes and likes/dislikes.

☐ Continue doing things that you enjoy and find meaningful as an individual.

☐ Develop and maintain an identity of your own.

CHAPTER 6
WHERE THERE'S A WILL

One hundred percent of us will die, but only 40 percent of us have prepared and signed a will. Maybe you're one of the 60 percent who probably know that you need a will, but just keep putting off writing one. Or maybe you think that you don't need one. After all, you're not rich, and whatever you have, your spouse will get. Or, the kids can fight over it after you're gone.

It won't matter to you then. But it will matter to your heirs.

Will Basics

Wills come in all varieties, and one or more would be appropriate for you, whatever your age or financial condition.

What is a will? Basically, it's a statement of what you want to happen to your property after your death. It can also determine who gets custody of your children, grandchildren, and even pets.

Who needs a will? Nearly everyone.

If you own property, if you have children, if you have anyone dependent on you for financial assistance, you need a will.

Some people superstitiously think making a will is inviting death. It's not. It's just being sensible. Most people think, "We'll get around to it someday, right after we clean out the garage, or finish that college course, or after we have our next checkup." Life is complicated, and we're all busy, but the few hours you spend watching football or browsing online would be enough time to handle the basics of a will.

Don't you want to have some say-so about what happens to all you've worked for? If you don't make a will, you are allowing someone else—the court or state legislature—to, in effect, make one for you, and it may not be at all what you'd have wanted.

I wrote my first will when I was waiting at a New York airport for an overseas flight, and mailed it to my sister. I was in my twenties and had only some books, silverware and a small savings account.

Later, when I married, my husband and I made "mirror" wills, leaving everything to each other. We also made bequests to other members of the family in case we died in a simultaneous incident such as an auto accident or a plane crash. When we had a child, we wrote new wills, including her and appointing guardians for her in case we both died before she reached 18.

Different States, Different Rules

When we moved to different states, we needed additional wills, as state laws on inheritance vary. Some states have a 'sweetheart' law, giving the surviving spouse the entire estate if there is no will. In others, the spouse gets part, while the remainder is divided among children, including children of prior marriages.

 Check your state laws regarding wills. Many states have brochures detailing what spousal rights apply. You can get these brochures at your local library, or from a lawyer or legal aid society.

How property is owned differs from state to state as well. For most couples, "Joint Ownership with Right of Survivorship" is the best way to take title to property. This means that the surviving spouse automatically owns the entire property without having to pay estate tax in most cases. It is usually assumed that all property acquired during a marriage is joint property, unless you specify otherwise. An example of this might be if one of you inherits property from your family and wants to keep it separate from jointly owned property.

In second marriages, property acquired during a lifetime with your former spouse could be automatically inherited by your second spouse unless you make some stipulation in a pre-nuptial agreement and in your will. For example, family antiques inherited by the husband might go to his widow, who then remarries. At her death, the items would pass to her second husband and his family. Is this what you want to happen to family items and other property?

Why Put It in Writing?

Why not just tell your family what you want done? Not a good idea. People who ordinarily get along well may quarrel when money is involved, and you won't be around to set things straight. And for tax reasons, it's better to leave real estate to your heirs by will rather than just putting their names on the deed.

Let's say you two bought a house years ago for $50,000, and after your husband's death you added your son's name as co-owner. By the time of your death, the house has increased in value to $200,000. If the son sells the property, he will have to pay capital gains tax on $150,000, the "profit" he made on a $50,000 house. On the other hand, if you will the house to your son and your estate is not valued at more than $1 million, he will not pay taxes upon inheriting it, and when he sells it, his tax base is $200,000. He would thus be taxed on any sales price above $200,000.

There are good reasons to put your wishes in writing. Louise, a widow, had put stickers on certain items with the names of the intended recipients, who were friends of hers. After her death her nephew turned the entire contents of her house over to an antique dealer and the stickers were overlooked or ignored.

 Give personal items away during your lifetime rather than leaving them by will. You can be sure they reach the intended person, and you can see that person enjoying your gift.

Otherwise, state clearly in your will who is to get what, in addition to putting stickers on the objects. It's also a good idea to take photos of the objects, and to let your executor know where the photos are located (for example, in a safe deposit box).

In another case, a farmer had two sons. He paid for the older to study dentistry while the younger remained at home and farmed. The younger was told that the farm would someday be his, but this was not put in writing. On the father's death, the farm was sold at the insistence of the older son and the proceeds divided equally between the two.

Fair? Of course not. Make certain your property is distributed as you want it to be. Put it in writing.

What Goes in a Will?

A will usually begins with your name, followed by stating

that you are of "sound mind" and that you are making this will freely.

 Next, name an executor, who may be your spouse, an adult child or other relative, or your lawyer. Choose a person younger than you as executor and one who resides in your state. Otherwise, your executor may have some difficulty qualifying or may refuse to serve because of travel difficulties and expenses.

Your executor will receive a fee for carrying out your wishes, usually 2 percent of your assets. There have been cases in which the executor charged a huge portion of the estate, leaving much less for the heirs, so choose the person carefully, get his or her consent to act, and name the person in your will.

 Then make your bequests. You cannot disinherit your spouse, but you can disinherit children or other relatives.

Give the full name of your spouse and your children and their birth dates. Then, if you wish to give less to one heir for some reason, you may say, for example, "I have provided for my son, Stephen Doe, by other means, and he is not to receive under this will."

 If you have minor children, state in your will who their guardians will be.

Choose two people, one to manage the child(ren)'s financial affairs and another to be their physical guardian, and these two should not be a married couple. Say, for example, that you choose your sister and her husband as guardians. The sister dies, your brother-in-law remarries and does not want to care for your child. Or the couple could divorce and want to live separate, different lives, with no resources for child care.

Discuss the guardianship with your chosen two, to make sure they are willing. After your death, if no one agrees to be guardians, the state will appoint as a guardian someone you might not approve of, or put your children into foster care.

Do you have pets? Sixty-three per cent of Americans have pets, but few of us have thought about the fate of our pets after our death.

 Ask friends and relatives if they would want Fluffy, and if so, mention this in your will, and leave that person a reasonable sum to assure Fluffy's care.

If you have no willing friends or relatives, ask at your local animal shelter or SPCA about foundations that care for pets. If you leave Fluffy to such a foundation, be prepared to make a bequest to the group. If you fail to provide for Fluffy, she will probably be taken to the nearest animal shelter and put up for adoption or euthanized.

 Just as with giving personal items, it's better to give to charities during your lifetime. You can take a tax deduction in addition to having the satisfaction of seeing your gift at work.

You also have the advantage of investigating the charity and giving according to its present program and needs. Charities change, and one that you support now may not even be around decades from now, or its goals may have changed from what you now support.

If you do leave a bequest to charity, it's better to leave it as a percentage of your estate, rather than a fixed amount. Your assets may decrease in value before your death, and if you have made a large bequest to a charity, your spouse and other heirs may have little left to live on.

If you want to donate to a charity but think your spouse will need the money during his/her lifetime, you might consider a charitable annuity, or leave the charitable gift to become effective on your spouse's death. Discuss this with your lawyer or financial adviser.

> When you write your will, make your spouse and other heirs aware of its general terms, so there are no unpleasant surprises after your death.

> Sign and date your will in the presence of witnesses. They should be younger than you are, so they're more likely to be around to verify that you signed freely and appeared to be of sound mind at the time. Don't have your spouse or any other heirs as witnesses. This could be grounds later for depriving that person of his/her share of your estate.

Yours and your spouse's wills should be prepared by a competent attorney, who will have a conference with both of you to discuss your wishes. Writing a will yourself is legal, and filling in a form purchased at a stationery store is cheap, but in the long run, money spent on having a valid will prepared is money saved for your heirs in avoiding litigation, fees and taxes later. A simple will should cost around $200, while a more complex one that might include one or more trusts would be $1,500 or more.

This is not a time to economize, but you can save on legal fees by being well prepared before your appointment with the lawyer.

> Bring with you the full names and dates of birth of your spouse and other heirs, a list of the assets you are bequeathing and any special conditions or statements you want included.

What Doesn't Go in Your Will?

 Don't include information about your funeral plans, your final illnesses or donations of body parts. Your will may not be read until some time after your death, and often not until after the funeral. By then it's too late to follow your wishes regarding disposition of your body.

 Don't include insurance policies. These go automatically to the beneficiary, which you should keep up to date. Don't include 401(k) savings accounts either. These go automatically to your spouse unless he/she signs a waiver giving up the right.

 Avoid making derogatory remarks about your heirs or putting conditions on inheritances, such as, "She will not inherit if she marries within a year of my death."

Where Should the Will Be Kept?

 Don't keep your will in your safe deposit box, as the box may be legally sealed at your death and not opened except by court order.

Put the original in a safe, accessible place in your home and let your executor and your spouse know the whereabouts of the will and the copies. Leave a copy with your lawyer or in the will vault of your bank, and send or give a sealed copy to your alternate executor.

 Destroy any previous wills.

Keep Your Will Current

1 Read over your will every year to make sure it reflects your present wishes and conditions.

You may need a new will for any of the following situations:

- You have been recently married, divorced or widowed.

- A child has been born or adopted into your family.

- One of your heirs has died.

- You have moved from one state to another.

- Your financial circumstances have changed sharply.

- You need to make special provisions for someone, such as care for a handicapped child.

- You decide to disinherit someone, include someone not mentioned previously in your will, or change the amount you are bequeathing to someone.

- You have simply changed your mind about some aspects of your will.

You should also have your lawyer prepare some other legal documents: a living will, which establishes what you want done if you are comatose or in the final stages of a terminal illness, a power of attorney for each of you, giving the other and an alternate the right to act for you when you are unable to, a medical care directive and possibly a trust. (These will be discussed in a later chapter.)

Checklist for Chapter 6

	Husband	Wife
Do you have a will?	☐	☐
Where is it?	☐	☐
Did your executor agree to serve?	☐	☐
Do you have minor children?	☐	☐
If so, have you chosen two guardians for them?	☐	☐
Have the guardians agreed to serve?	☐	☐
Do your heirs know the general terms of your will?	☐	☐
If you have a pet/pets, have you made provision for it/them?	☐	☐
If you have set up a trust, have the trustees agreed to serve?	☐	☐
Are your heirs aware of the Trust?	☐	☐
If your will was written more than two years ago, have you re-read it within the past six months? If not, do so.	☐	☐

CHAPTER 7
"WE NEED TO TALK"

When someone says, "We need to talk," most of us tense, expecting bad news. It usually means we've done something unacceptable and are due for a scolding, or a relationship is about to end. Helen Gurley Brown wrote about inviting her husband to meet her for lunch to discuss something crucial. He went half-expecting to hear that she wanted a divorce. Instead, she wanted him to lose weight, a sensitive enough subject, but not as bad as what he feared. He was so relieved that he agreed to a checkup and a diet.

 Your conversations with your mate should take place when issues come up, not avoided until the situation has reached crisis proportions and/or when one of you expects the proverbial ax to fall.

 Be open and honest in discussing important topics that affect your relationship.

We sometimes "let sleeping dogs lie," sidestepping controversies to keep the peace at any price. We drift along, talking only of superficial things with our mate while the discontent simmers and builds until we strike out with harsh words that poison our relationships.

Some immature people walk around sulking in silence, waiting for the other to ask what's wrong. Their response, "If you don't know, I won't tell you." Or, "If you loved me, you'd know." Your spouse is not a mind reader. Say what's bothering you, in a calm, non-accusatory voice. If you're too angry to be calm and logical, say so, and set a time to discuss the issue.

How to Start a Tough Conversation

Marriage counselors have developed a set of suggestions for productive marital conversations, and these may help you:

- Choose a time when you both are rested and ready to concentrate, not distracted by sports, ringing phones, etc.

- Don't keep bringing up the same old issues and accusations. Stick to the present topic. If necessary, write down the topic for discussion, state how you resolved the issue, date it and file it.

- Look at each other and listen carefully, without interrupting. When the other has finished speaking, state what you think you heard. Use phrases like "I feel that—" instead of "You always..." For example, you might say, "I feel that you don't value the time I spend cleaning when you drop your dirty clothes on the floor for me to pick up," instead of "You're such a slob! I don't know why I married you."

- Find a place where you won't be interrupted. It may be at home, in a nearby park, or in a restaurant or a similar place. In bed is probably not the best place. Counselors say bed should be for sleep and sex, not quarrels.

If you can't discuss issues calmly and rationally as a pair, you may need to air your issues in the presence of a marriage counselor, a spiritual advisor or a close, trusted friend.

What issues are you likely to discuss? This will change as the length and circumstances of your marriage change. In the early years, you'll need to settle the matters of budgeting, birth control, sharing of tasks, relationships with each other's families, where to live and religious preferences.

Remember your dating days, when you spent hours getting to know each other, only to discover later that there were important things you forgot to ask or never considered would matter? Bring up those subjects now and hash them out.

Finances

Talking about finances can be some of the toughest conversations you'll ever have in your marriage, but both of you should always be honest about your finances and your financial goals. When do you want to retire? Where? What do you want to do with the rest of your life when your working days are past?

Do you have any debts, such as student loans or credit card charges that you've been keeping from each other? A surprise like this can ruin your credit rating as a couple and may ruin your relationship as well. Almost as disruptive is keeping a secret stash or bank account.

 Discuss and agree on how to pay off debts and how to save money for your future.

Write down each suggestion, no matter how unlikely it seems at the time. Both spouses should have a certain amount of money to spend, no questions asked. This was never a problem for Tom and me. We both were employed for most of our marriage, and whatever we earned or inherited went into our joint account, from which bills were paid. We took turns writing checks to pay bills.

Renee and her husband had a similar system. They discussed all money matters, including charitable donations, regular expenses, stock purchases, etc. so she knew where they stood financially. She also knew what he was leaving to her and what to his children from a previous marriage.

One bit of advice for couples from John Hundley, who is widowed: make sure you both know how to balance the checkbook, keep it up to date and always keep some cash on hand. Both of you should know where the money is and have agreed on its amount (see Chapter 3, "What Are You Worth?").

Marty Hines's husband Anthony was an accountant, and during tax-filing season he'd put his effort into preparing other people's taxes, not their own. He'd make sure they were due a refund, then wait and file three years' worth of returns at once. He didn't confide to Marty what he was doing, which resulted in her getting a warning letter from IRS after his death.

Health

Health also needs discussing early in a relationship. Obvious issues include exposure to sexually transmitted diseases and a family history of hereditary conditions that may shorten your life or affect your decision to have children.

After you've been married a few years, the issues are more likely to involve child care and discipline, decision-making, family priorities and possibly the illness of one of you or a member of your families.

As your life together continues, different issues will arise that you need to discuss. Do you foresee the two of you moving into a retirement home at some point? What if one of you becomes incapacitated? Should you purchase long term care insurance and/or investigate assisted-living facilities?

Later, if one of you is seriously ill, you'll have a different kind of conversations. Are the financial, legal, medical and practical matters covered in this book taken care of? What kind of living arrangements are necessary during this illness? Afterward?

In later years, you'll probably want and need to settle end-of-life choices, express your love for each other often and even talk about how each of you will cope without the other. If you have a good relationship, you would probably want your beloved to be happy after you are gone, to "go out into the world," make new friends and eventually find love again.

Decisions

At any stage of a marriage, there are emotional issues, often resulting from decisions made without both partners' involvement. Marilyn confided an instance when her husband Bradley loaned their second car without consulting her. "One of his colleagues wrecked his car and his wife needed it to drive to her job. Without asking me, Brad offered ours, leaving me at home pregnant with no transportation. We lived a couple of blocks from a bus stop, but that's not the point.

"When the car was returned, it had minor damage. Instead of having it repaired, they gave us a check for the deductible, so we had to put it on our insurance. The colleague didn't like Brad any better for having made the loan. He was just played for a sucker. Brad saw he'd been wrong to lend the car, but he never apologized and we never discussed it. If I had it to do over, I'd have said, 'You did what? Well, you can just tell them it's your wife's car and she needs it. Let them rent one.'"

Peggy had a similar experience. Her husband Karl's aunt needed a place to live as her building had been condemned, and she'd put off finding a place. Without asking Peggy, Karl arranged for his aunt to move into their guest room and share meals.

"She paid us room and board, so she wasn't a financial burden, but her being there was all wrong. We had a small child and a dog and she didn't like children or animals. It was supposed to be just until she could find a place, but it dragged on until she had a fall and needed to go to a nursing home. By that time, she and I were hardly speaking. That was the worst period of our marriage. Karl and I should definitely have discussed this and agreed on it—from my point of view, agreeing that his aunt would be limited to one month, which was plenty of time for her to find a place of her own."

Secrets

My original title of this chapter was "No Secrets," and it's important that both partners feel free and open with each other. But the word "secrets" is divisive and negative, and positive conversations are what you want and should aim for.

> Each partner should reveal everything of consequence to the other. Children you haven't mentioned, a criminal record, a problem with your citizenship, past name changes—if you're scared to admit it to anyone, you should probably tell your partner about it.

A real shocker would be discovering that your deceased spouse had children you weren't aware of. They may come forward to claim a share of your estate, and so may imposters. Be honest about their existence now, with all the information you have about them. This will protect your survivors against false claims. If there are no such secret offspring, note in your will that "X, Y and Z are my only children," and list their birth dates.

Have you ever been convicted of a crime? It would be devastating to have this come out after keeping it a secret for a long time. Your spouse would be unlikely to ever trust you again.

 Be honest as well in admitting incorrect information, something you have bragged about that isn't true, whether military distinction, degrees or accomplishments.

For example, for years a man claimed that he had written the song "Yellow Polka Dot Bikini." His family mentioned it in his obituary and the news was picked up by national TV. Imagine his family's embarrassment when the real composer saw the news and came forward with his copyright proof.

The Important Things

Not all your conversations should be serious or potentially devastating. Spend time recalling happy memories, even while you are making other good memories. Take a walk together on a sunny afternoon, or sit outside on a starry night or chat beside a fire on a damp, wet day. Talk of your hopes and dreams and how glad you are to be with each other.

 Ask each other "What is really important to you in life?" and "What issues are unresolved?"

A friend confessed after the death of his wife of 37 years, "We talked a lot in her last months and weeks, but there were some things unresolved, things we should have worked on earlier." I couldn't help wondering about the issues they hadn't resolved, and why. He was too full of grief and regret at the time, and by now has probably forgotten telling me that. Or maybe they were just too busy living and loving that those issues didn't matter.

If you have the luxury of a "last conversation" with your spouse, be present with all your senses and let the words flow naturally. It is too late to discuss unresolved issues, nor is it the time to clear your conscience by confessing to some wrong that will only hurt your dying spouse or the survivor. Reaffirm your love and ensure a calm environment. Whether at home or in a hospital, ask others to leave you two alone for a few minutes. Let your spouse say whatever comes to his/her mind, without undue coaxing on your part.

On a website for widows, one woman wrote, "If only wives knew what widows know." She said that if she could go back to before, she'd listen to her husband's problems more, scold and nag him less, try harder to get along with his family, and show her love more affectionately.

You may not have the opportunity in those final hours to tell your beloved how much you care, so say it now.

Checklist for Chapter 7

☐ Talk about issues with your mate when they come up. Don't avoid the topic until the situation has reached crisis proportions and/or when one of you expects the proverbial ax to fall.

☐ Always be open and honest in discussing important topics that affect your relationship.

☐ Discuss and agree on how to pay off debts and how to save money for your future.

☐ Talk about any health issues that come up depending on your age and individual circumstances.

☐ Don't make any major decisions without your partner's input; if your partner has made such a decision without you, speak up and make sure your needs are taken into consideration.

☐ Don't keep secrets from your spouse. The longer a secret is kept, the more devastating it is when the truth inevitably comes out.

☐ Talk about the "big picture" of life: what matters most to each other, what brings each of you the most joy.

☐ Learn as much as you can about your partner, and share as much as you can about yourself.

CHAPTER 8
IN SICKNESS AND HEALTH

When you married, you agreed to stay together "in sickness and in health." In a perfect world, you would experience only health, but that's not the way things are. You will have sickness. It's lurking there. You need to prepare for it, and at the same time do all you can to prevent it.

Health Insurance

 My advice to anyone getting married is two-fold: both of you should have a thorough physical exam, and you should buy health insurance.

Many young healthy people play the odds and figure they'll buy health insurance later. We're all one slip-and-fall or one diagnosis away from gigantic medical bills. The older we get the more certain this outcome is, but it can happen at any age, and you don't want to leave your mate bankrupt because of your illness.

The most economical kind of health insurance has a high deductible: that is, you will pay for your own doctor's bills and drugs up to your deductible amount. The insurance will cover about 80 percent of the costs above the deductible. This protects you against catastrophic costs, much as you have automobile insurance to cover accidents and lawsuits, but not ordinary maintenance, such as oil changes.

When you reach 65, you'll be eligible for Medicare, but you'll still need supplementary insurance, referred to as MediGap.

Disability Insurance

> *If you are employed and have the opportunity to buy disability insurance at a reasonable price, by all means do so.*

Also, be wary of working for an employer who does not have disability insurance on his employees. Teddy was always willing to help a friend or family member, and when an ice storm broke up trees in his brother's yard, Teddy got out his chain saw and went to help. As he freed one limb, another fell on him, crushing his lower body. He was paralyzed from the waist down, and neither he nor his brother had disability insurance. Teddy and his wife had to give up their house to pay the first set of medical bills, and she eventually divorced him so he could qualify for Medicaid to give him continuing care.

Disability insurance usually pays not only medical bills, but replaces lost income for a set length of time, as we hear from the Aflac duck on TV.

Dental Insurance

> *Dental insurance is another type of coverage that many people don't think about—until they need it—but I recommend that everyone have it.*

Few people have dental insurance unless it comes as part of

a group insurance package. I had it for years through my employer but had little need of it. Then as I got older, things began to fall apart: the mercury fillings from my teen years, the bridge that replaced a tooth knocked out at summer camp. By this time I was covered by my ex-husband's policy, so the fillings and bridge were replaced. I also needed a couple of root canals and endured them.

Both the marriage and the dental coverage came to an end. I had the opportunity to get dental insurance for $35 more per month added onto my insurance policy, but I declined. After all, I'd had everything taken care of. Four months later, I broke a tooth eating popcorn and faced a bill of $1,200, which I had to pay out of pocket.

Long Term Care Insurance

This type of insurance is controversial: should you buy it or not? By the time most people decide they need such insurance, they can't qualify or think it's too expensive. Insurers are no fools. If you're 85 and having difficulty breathing, they know you'll soon be needing care, and they don't want you as a customer.

If you have over a million dollars in assets, you can afford whatever kind of nursing care you want. If you have less than $100,000, you'll soon run out of money and will then qualify for Medicaid. My situation put me in the middle group, neither rich enough nor poor enough. Most financial advisers tell people that long-term care insurance (LTC) is for people like me, in the middle.

My then-husband had had LTC for years, and insisted that I buy it so I would not be a burden on him or cause us to lose the house, so I applied. A nurse came to our home to interview, weigh and measure me. She got a complete medical history and gave me a mental test using flashcards, to make sure I didn't have Alzheimer's.

I qualified and bought coverage for three years of nursing home care, which is the average length of stay in an LTC facility. It cost more than $4,000 a year, and the premiums went up each year. When my ex and I were divorced, I let the policy lapse and am keeping what I would have paid for the policy in a special account. I am not a burden on anyone else now. However, your experience may be quite different from mine.

 As a couple, you need to discuss this and arrive at a decision that suits you both. The average cost of a nursing home now is more than $75,000 per year. Can you afford this? For how long?

Medivac Insurance and Traveling Healthy

 If you travel overseas, you should probably buy medical evacuation insurance.

I have had this insurance for years and have never needed to file a claim, so I can't give assurances of how good it is—and hope I never have to find out. I was told of a passenger on a cruise ship who suffered a heart attack. The ship's doctor treated him first, then summoned a helicopter to take the patient ashore to a Mexican hospital. From there, he was flown back to his hometown. The total cost was more than $50,000, even before the treatment in his hospital back home.

It's comforting to know that if you're gored by a bull or contract a tropical disease, you can be flown back to your own doctor for treatment. It's even more comforting if insurance pays most of the cost.

The cost of medical travel insurance depends on a number of factors: your age, the length of your trip and the dollar amount of coverage you want. Note: Medicare does not cover you in foreign countries. Your travel agent or AAA can sell you such policies, or recommend a company. Two such companies are www.TravelInsuranceCenter.com/Select and www.wallach. com.

 Before you leave on a trip, find out from your local health department or www.CDC.gov what shots are needed, and get them.

If you're advised to take malaria prevention tablets, have your physician write a prescription for such pills and take them according to directions. I had a narrow escape with Larium, an anti-malarial drug. The physician wrote that I was to take the pills daily, beginning a week before my trip and continuing through the trip and for a week afterward. If I had followed his directions, I would not have survived to make the trip. Luckily, I'd taken Larium before and recognized the pills. I remembered that I was to take them weekly, and checked with CDC to make sure this was the same dosage I'd taken before. I had far too many pills, and wasted my money, but at least I didn't overdose.

Be sure to pack your medications as well as spare eyeglasses and a listing of all the medications you're taking, with their generic names. In many countries drugs are sold over the counter without prescription, provided you have the generic name. Your luggage may be lost or stolen, and if you need to take medications on a regular basis, you can't wait until you get back home to get a new prescription.

If you have a chronic condition or allergies to medications, you should consider getting and wearing a Medic Alert bracelet to alert anyone giving you emergency care. The bracelet or a medical insurance card should include your condition, your doctor's name and phone number, and medications you are taking.

 Whether you are healthy or sick, you should carry a card headed "In Case of Emergency, Please Notify."

Then list at least three people with their phone numbers and their relationship to you. You may also have their numbers programmed into your cell phone, under the heading ICE ("in case of emergency"). In addition, if you have had your blood typed, carry a card stating this. It will save valuable time if you are in an accident and need a transfusion.

Keeping Healthy

In addition to insurance you both should be taking care of your health.

 Know what health conditions each of you has, who your doctors are, how often they are to be consulted, what medications you are each taking and how often.

 Prepare a medical history for each of you (this is covered in Chapter 11, "Making a List, Checking it Twice").

It's possible to continue living a full life even with health issues and disabilities, but it does take some extra effort by the partner. My friend Linda Kunz led an active life despite three-times-per-week kidney dialysis, and my friend Fran Byers traveled the world with her husband who also needed dialysis. They located dialysis centers around the world and planned their trips to be near a center on the day dialysis was needed.

Your home can help keep you healthy or harm you.

Study your home and answer the following questions:

- Is it situated so that each of you could manage to care for the other?

- Do you have easily accessible bathing facilities, including a shower seat and hand-held shower?

- Are doorways wide enough for wheelchairs?

- Do the doors have levers instead of knobs, to make them easier to open?

- Are steps at a minimum?

- If the house is more than one story, are there a bedroom and bath on the main floor?

- Are floor surfaces free of clutter and rugs that might cause a fall?

More important than the house is what goes on within it. Look after each other's health as well as you can. No one will lose weight or give up smoking until he/she is ready to, but you can make a joint effort if you share the same condition. Most of us would benefit from eating fewer sweets and fats, and more fruits and vegetables. If your spouse is making an effort to improve his/her health, offer encouragement and compliments, but don't monitor or micromanage them. You want to keep your loving mate with you as long as possible, but you don't want to alienate them in the process.

 Well before either of you becomes incapacitated, discuss what you want done for you in your final days, and record your decisions.

Chapter 9, "Put It in Writing" covers end-of-life documents. Complete your own and distribute copies to doctors and family members who need to know.

When an illness is terminal, consider hospice care. I can't say enough good things about the caring people who give their time to look after and cheer those whose death is imminent— and their survivors.

If you are the survivor, you'll know that you did the best you could for your beloved.

Checklist for Chapter 8

☐ Both of you should have a thorough physical exam, and you should buy health insurance.

☐ If you are employed and have the opportunity to buy disability insurance at a reasonable price, by all means do so.

☐ If you can get dental insurance at a reasonable price, do so.

☐ Discuss long term care insurance and determine if it's a good idea for you as a couple.

☐ If you travel overseas, you should probably buy medical evacuation insurance.

☐ Before you leave on a trip, find out from your local health department or www.CDC.gov what shots are needed, and get them.

☐ If you have a chronic condition or allergies to medications, you should consider getting and wearing a Medic Alert bracelet.

☐ Carry a card headed "In Case of Emergency, Please Notify" with the names and phone number of three people to contact in case of an emergency.

☐ Program the emergency contact information into your cell phone under the name ICE ("in case of emergency")

☐ Know what health conditions each of you has, who your doctors are, how often they are to be consulted, what medications you are each taking and how often.

☐ Evaluate your home for how easily you could live there if you were disabled.

☐ Well before either of you becomes incapacitated, discuss what you want done for you in your final days, and record your decisions.

CHAPTER 9
PUT IT IN WRITING

Documenting your wishes for the disposition of your estate involves a lot of big legal decisions, and you'll never know whether you've done everything right. But your spouse and heirs will. As Albert Crenshaw wrote in *The Virginian-Pilot*, "the problem with estate planning is that you're never done with it, at least not while you're alive."

You may have thought that once you'd made a will, you'd taken care of legal matters, but there are several other documents that are almost as important. They may, in fact, be more important during your lifetime. These documents are power of attorney, living will (or health care power of attorney), health care directive and trusts.

Power of Attorney

A power of attorney is a legal document giving someone else the power to act for you when you are unable to do so. The document must be prepared and signed while you are in good mental and physical health. It will then become effective after a "triggering event," such as a stroke or disabling accident.

However, you need not be ill to need a power of attorney. You may want to turn your legal and financial affairs over to someone else when you are away from your usual residence. For example, when members of the armed forces are deployed, they usually designate a spouse or family member to act on their behalf and give them a power of attorney.

A power of attorney may be "general durable" or "limited." A limited one spells out specific duties the "attorney in fact" is to do, or it is in effect for a limited time. Before Brad and Connie were married, they bought a house in Georgia, near her home. He was living in California, and to avoid flying across the continent to sign the real estate closing papers, he gave her a limited power of attorney. That power of attorney was good for that day only and for that specific purpose.

A general durable power of attorney is far-reaching, as its name implies. It lists the powers granted, but the first one pretty well summarizes its extent: "to transact all business and personal affairs for me."

Following this there is a listing of powers: to collect money, sign checks and notes, pay bills, withdraw funds from bank accounts, borrow money, lease or sell real estate, pay medical personnel, receive confidential information and deal with courts and legal agencies. The document concludes that the designated person should "do and perform as I myself would or could if acting personally."

The general durable power of attorney is thus substituting someone else for you in all matters. This person could wreak havoc with your life if he or she had evil intent, and so you must choose your "attorney" carefully. Fortunately, a power of attorney doesn't become active unless you want it to.

 If you decide to create a power of attorney, it should be prepared by a lawyer, signed and put in your file cabinet or some other safe place where it can be found and used when it's needed.

A copy should be given or sent to the person you have designated as your "attorney in fact."

You may give a power of attorney to more than one person, and you should state in the document that the second person named is in addition to the first. Tom and I gave each other our power of attorney and designated my sister as an additional "attorney in fact."

A power of attorney can be revoked at any time you wish, simply by destroying all copies of the document. Before you destroy your power of attorney, you should have another drawn up and ready for signature. It is a good idea to have *someone* designated as your "attorney in fact" at all times. You never know what life will bring.

Since your power of attorney usually would not become effective until there is a "triggering event" in your life, the designated "attorney in fact" may need a statement from a doctor as to your condition. The power of attorney allows him to acquire confidential information, but *not* until he has become the "attorney in fact." This little catch-22 can be by-passed with an additional, one-page form giving your proposed "attorney in fact" the authority to receive your medical information.

A health care power of attorney applies to all medical decisions made on your behalf, not just whether or how to end your life, and it names a health care agent to act for you when you are unable to do so. This person can receive information from your doctor(s) and hospital that would otherwise be prohibited by recent privacy laws, and can authorize medical treatments, including x-rays, other tests and medications.

In choosing someone as your health care agent, it should be someone you trust to follow your wishes. It should not be your medical care provider, for obvious reasons; nor your spouse, who may be too emotional where you are concerned; or your heirs, who may have reasons of their own to reject your wishes.

 You should also carry in your wallet a "code status" card that also includes the name and phone number of your health care agent.

He or she will be aware of your wishes. You may also want to post on your refrigerator or some other prominent spot a brightly colored notice expressing your code wishes in case medical emergency personnel have to be summoned to your home.

 Like all legal documents, it's a good idea to have an attorney prepare the power of attorney so that it complies with the laws of your state.

Living Wills and Health Care Directives

After the Terry Schiavo case, in which a young woman lived in a vegetative state for 15 years, many Americans suddenly gave thought to how their final days were to be lived and ended. You probably want to spare your survivors the anguish and expense of such a tragic situation. If you put your wishes in writing, your spouse and other survivors will feel secure in carrying out what you want.

A document stating that you do not wish to be kept alive by artificial means when there is little or no hope of recovery is usually called a living will. An example of such a document can be found at www.caring-info.org/stateaddownload.

Living wills have been upheld by courts in all states, though their wording differs from state to state, and so does what they are called. For instance, in North Carolina such a document is called "A Declaration of a Desire for a Natural Death."

 You should discuss having a living will with your

spouse or partner and other heirs, and *put it in writing.*

Use the sample document linked above as a template.

You may want both a living will and a health care power of attorney. If you do, they should be prepared as part of the same document to avoid conflict or differing interpretations.

Trusts

Trusts may be used in addition to wills or in place of wills. One advantage of a trust is that property already in the trust will pass to heirs without the necessity of probate. Wills that are probated become public, so that anyone who wishes can go to the courthouse Will Book and read the details of your bequests. Not so a trust.

Setting up a trust is not a do-it-yourself project; it must be handled by an attorney. Trusts may be either revocable, meaning you can make changes whenever you wish, or irrevocable, which are not changeable. Trusts are used to transfer large estates, sometimes bypassing one's children and settling bequests on grandchildren.

They may be set up to provide steady, guaranteed income for someone who is incapable of providing it for him- or herself. For example, if you have a handicapped child, you would want to make sure that he/she is well cared-for and does not become destitute. Or, you may feel that one of your heirs does not handle money well and might need the protection of a steady stream of income rather than a lump sum which could soon be exhausted.

The bulk of your assets will be in the trust, which will pass to the survivor with a minimum of fuss and taxes. One of the main purposes of this book is to prepare both you and your spouse to function on your own after the death of the other, and that includes managing your money. You will need to consult a financial adviser to determine if a trust would benefit you.

The trustee, or person who handles the money for someone else, may be a lawyer, a bank official, or a dependable relative. For large or complicated estates, the trustee may be a group of people.

Five Wishes

Thirty-six states and the District of Columbia now recognize the Five Wishes form, a 10-page document that has a series of questions, instructions and fill-in blanks for you to designate a health care agent and express your choice for your end-of-life treatment.

 You can get a copy of this at your local hospital, at www.agingwithdignity.com or by writing Aging With Dignity, P. O. Box 1661, Tallahassee, FL, 32302-1661, or by calling 888-594-7437.

 Once you have filled it in and signed it before two witnesses, make multiple copies.

File a copy with your personal physician or medical center, and give a copy to your attorney. Your spouse, designated as next of kin, should have a copy, and you should include a copy in your medical records file.

If you already have a living will and a health care power of attorney, you may use the Five Wishes instead. Simply destroy these two documents after you have signed Five Wishes. If you later change your mind about what you have stated in Five Wishes, complete another form and destroy the first.

This group and its brochure are intended for elderly people. If you live in a state that does not recognize this form, or if you are younger and might therefore have different priorities or wishes, you can pick up a brochure at your local library describing living wills in your state. Everyone over the age of 18 should have a living will prepared and signed, or should complete and sign Five Wishes. You never know when disaster might strike. After all, Terry Schiavo was only 26 when she went into an irreversible coma.

> ⚡ In deciding what kind of end-of-life care you might want to receive, consider the possibility of pregnancy, whether you want your organs donated, and what "code" you want followed for do not resuscitate (DNR).

My niece included in her document that if she were pregnant and in the third trimester, she would wish to be kept alive until the child could be delivered safely. Also, if you intend to be an organ donor, medical personnel might keep you "alive" long enough to keep your organs viable. Making your wishes clear will spare your survivors grief and heartache, and the cost of a lawsuit to defend themselves against those who might disagree with your choices.

"Full code" for DNR means that you want all lifesaving and supportive measures unless your condition fails to improve. At that point, the provisions of your living will or Five Wishes will go into effect. You may choose "full code except for cardiac arrest," meaning you do not want your stopped heart restarted. Or you may choose "comfort or hospice care," with no extraordinary measures taken. The questions in Five Wishes allow you to state your preferences on these matters and to make additional comments or requests.

Before having a lawyer prepare your health care power of

attorney or writing your own, or completing Five Wishes, you may want to get up-to-date information and sample forms from Concern for Dying or the Society for the Right to Die, both at 250 West 57th Street, New York, NY 10107.

After discussing your medical wishes with your spouse and other heirs, discuss them also with your family doctor. You may find that your doctor disagrees philosophically with what you want and would not follow your written instructions. In this case, you should seriously consider finding a new doctor. Otherwise, your last days may be the scene of ugly wrangling, distressing to your spouse and possibly expensive if a lawsuit ensues.

To prevent quarrels among your survivors and unnecessary, lengthy suffering for you, put your wishes in writing. Today. This is not about money. It's your life.

Checklist for Chapter 9

☐ If you decide to create a power of attorney, it should be prepared by a lawyer, signed and put in your file cabinet or some other safe place where it can be found and used when it's needed.

☐ Discuss having a living will with your spouse or partner and other heirs, then complete a living will using an appropriate template for your state, available online.

☐ Consider using a "Five Wishes" form, if that form is approved for use by your state.

☐ In deciding what kind of end-of-life care you might want to receive, consider the possibility of pregnancy, whether you want your organs donated, and what "code" you want followed for do not resuscitate (DNR).

CHAPTER 10
KEEPING TABS

Is your desk covered with sliding piles of paper? Mine often is. Do you waste time searching for something you've put in a "safe place"? I do. I'm good about hanging up clothes, running the dishwasher and scooping my cat's litter box, but filing is one of my dreaded and thus postponed tasks.

Anybody can file. All you have to do is put papers into a folder and stick a label on it. The trick is finding those papers again. Filing has to be logical and organized, or it's less than worthless.

When I worked as an administrative assistant at the University of Texas, my boss would drop a handful of papers on my desk and say, "File them." I'd nod and smile and start worrying. File them where? Is there already a file for this subject? If there is, what is it called? Worse, if there isn't, how do I know what to name this one so I—or whoever got my job after I was fired—could find it?

As far as I know, I never goofed—at least, not on filing.

Filing is easier with your own home situation, because you probably know what titles to give your files. However, filing is still necessary for most of us. In spite of computer advances that let you scan documents and record electronically everything you send out, you'll probably still need to keep letters, receipts, guarantees and other pieces of paper that others generate and send to you. And you'll certainly want to keep original legal documents, such as deeds, marriage licenses, birth certificates and contracts, as well as paid bills and various warranties.

Most important, you should be able to lay your hands on whatever documents you need quickly. If you can't find a particular piece of paper, think how much more frustrating it would be for your survivors when you're not around to suggest likely places to search.

Before You Start Filing

If you don't have a filing system, or if yours is chaotic, I'm afraid it's time to bite the bullet.

⚡ Get a place to put all your papers.

Depending on how many papers you have, your filing needs might be met by a portable file box, or you might require a full-size filing cabinet. If you're unsure where to start, consider getting a used two-drawer filing cabinet from an office-supply closeout store. The more heavy-duty of a filing cabinet you can get, the better; a piece of paper is light, but hundreds of them together weigh *a lot*.

⚡ Get your filing supplies.

You'll need hanging file folders (again, sturdier is better), a few individual manila folders for the larger categories like Insurance, labels for both types of folders and, if you like a tidy, uniform look to your filing system, a label-maker. You can also use a dark marker or pen, or prepare labels on your computer.

⚡ Gather all your papers together.

All the stacks that have built up around the house, all the

papers you've tucked into drawers or boxes or even suitcases over the years, that pile of mail on the table next to the door.

 Clear out some space to work.

Put your filing cabinet in the space you intend it to stay, and make some space around it. Borrow some folding tables from a friend and set up a lot of open space to sort your papers as you prepare to file them.

 Dedicate time for filing.

For most of us, this is a lengthy task, so you'll want to set aside at least half a day. It's discouraging and unproductive to get started and then have to put everything back and start another time.

 Don't file anything you don't need.

Sort through the papers you've gathered, discarding old papers, such as expired offers. Keep two bags handy for discarded papers: one for papers that may safely be recycled and a second for papers that have identifying information, such as Social Security numbers, and must be shredded.

 Try to make it fun.

Move a TV or CD player into the room where you're doing your filing to keep you entertained during the process. Filing doesn't require a whole lot of brainpower so you can watch or listen to something you enjoy without losing very much efficacy in the filing. Just be sure to stay on task with your filing, using the entertainment as a pleasant accompaniment. Or consider asking a friend to help you with the filing, especially if you can then help the friend set up his or her filing system.

What to File

So, what categories do you need for your filing system?

Legal Documents

A must for every household. This will include birth certificates, marriage licenses, divorce decrees, military separation papers, Social Security cards (don't carry the originals with you), a copy of your Last Will and Testament, powers of attorney, car titles and information on any lawsuits you may be involved in. Unless you travel a lot and have a separate folder for travel, your passport should also go in this folder.

Financial Records

This will hold your estate plan if you have made one, trust documents, retirement accounts such as IRAs, brokerage statements, bank statements and loans you have made to others, loans that you owe and proof that loans have been paid. Personally, I don't keep my brokerage and bank statements in a folder, but in a 3-ring binder kept on the bookshelf.

Charge Accounts

Since I have several charge cards, I have a folder labeled "Charge Accounts," with separate inner folders for MasterCard, Visa and American Express. Individual charge slips go into marked envelopes. When the bills arrive, I match charges to statements, pay the bills and file the statements with the date noted on which it was paid. Most charge slips will be tossed or shredded, unless it is for some taxable item.

Homeowner File

Here you'll file the real estate closing papers for your home purchase, the amortization statement showing how many more payments you must make on your mortgage, what portion is interest vs. principal and other records relating to the purchase itself. Deeds to your property should be filed in the local courthouse and a copy kept in your safe deposit box. Leases on rental property should be in your home file cabinet. If you rent instead of owning your residence, a copy of your lease should be filed.

Home Repairs

This is different from the purchase papers. This file includes documents relating to replacing a roof, renovating or adding space, having a new heating system or water heater installed, etc. This will come in handy when you sell your home. If you pay for these items by check, file a copy of the bank statement showing payment along with the paid bill. If you pay by credit card, staple the charge slip to the itemized bill. This information is also useful if something you have paid for is unsatisfactory. You'll have proof of the date and the amount.

Medical

This file should include a medical history for each of you, your blood type, lists of medications you're taking, prescriptions for eyeglasses and/or hearing aids, the results of medical tests and bills from doctors, hospitals or insurance companies. Your copy of the Five Wishes form or your medical power of attorney and living will may be kept here. They can also be electronically registered and stored at www.google.com/intl/en/health/advance-directive.html. Or, they and other legal documents may be recorded at www.DocuBank.com.

Insurance

Within a large folder, keep separate folders for the various types of insurance you may have: homeowners, auto, life, health, medical evacuation, long-term care, liability or umbrella, and personal property. The policy for each should go in the file, along with recent bills and contact information for each company. If you have certain personal items insured, such as jewelry, you'll need to keep the appraisals in this file also.

Taxes

Pay stubs, royalty statements and other evidence of income will be in this folder, along with a copy of last year's tax return and the slips you need to send if you make estimated tax payments. Your tax folder will also hold proof of deductions, such as letters thanking you for charitable contributions and a log book recording miles driven for business or charitable purposes.

Bills to Pay

Unless you have all your bills paid automatically by your bank, you will need a file that holds incoming bills. As you open a bill, note the date it is due, and arrange your file with the bills needing to be paid soonest at the front. It's also helpful to have a list of when certain bills are due to arrive and when they are to be paid. This way, if a bill is late arriving, you can call to make sure someone else is not intercepting your mail and possibly stealing your identity. Similarly, if you know you are going to be away at the time the bill arrives, you can arrange to pay ahead of time.

Filing bills properly—and paying on time—will keep you from incurring late penalties. I learned this the hard way when

I missed paying a Visa bill before its due date. The amount charged was only $24, but the "late penalty" was $25 and "interest" was $2. The interest rate was thus 100 percent annually, and the penalty was more than 100 percent.

Utilities

Although I have my utilities paid by the bank, I receive paper notifications, and I check them for accuracy. This enabled me to notice that my water bill had jumped an alarming amount. At my sister's suggestion, I ran tests, determined that I had a leaking toilet and replaced it. Keeping utility bills for two years makes it easy to determine savings if you've had energy-efficient items installed.

Children

If you have children, you should have a file on each one. In it, record the child's birthday, which school he/she is enrolled in, what grade and the teacher's name. (You know all of this information, of course, but this fill will be incredibly helpful for others.) You may also want to keep report cards, awards won and even samples of artwork, once they have been displayed on the fridge. In my file on Catherine, I also have cards she made for me and a fledgling "newspaper" she wrote one summer. Take frequent photos of your child and always have a recent one available, as well as the names of your child's friends, in case something happens to your child.

Pets

If you have a pet or pets, you'll need a file for each, labeled with the pet's name. Into the folder go when and where you acquired the pet, checkups with the vet, licenses and proof of rabies shots and lineage papers if the pet is purebred. And if your cat is as determined to lose collars with nametags as mine is, have several tags made when you're at the pet shop, and keep extras in the file.

Consider having an identifying computer chip implanted under your pet's skin. Collars can be lost or removed, but a microchip can't. If your pet is lost or stolen, the chip will provide identity. Animal shelters, vets and animal control personnel know to look for it.

Addresses

Into this folder go the church directory, club membership lists and a printout of the addresses of people to whom I send my annual Christmas message. (The list is also on the computer, and is updated when necessary, as people move, divorce or die.) I also have a Rolodex of addresses and phone numbers and a separate file of email addresses. People I email regularly are on my computer as "Contacts," but there are other addresses I may want to use, just not often.

In the Event of my Death

This folder will include deeds to cemetery plots, receipts and details for pre-paid funerals, your pre-written obituary and funeral plans.

Additional Folders

I have additional files that you may not want or need. I'm a writer, a traveler and a member of various organizations, plus I own a timeshare and live in a community that has an active civic association. I have folders for each.

Travel

This folder includes my passport, international immunization card, printouts of upcoming itineraries, brochures and coupons for possible future trips.

Neighborhood/Homeowners Association

My Neighborhood folder holds the association's by-laws and rules as well as schedules of several interest groups I'm involved in.

Associations

This folder holds information on airline and hotel loyalty programs as well as other clubs I belong to, such as AAA, Friends of the Library and my church.

Timeshare

This folder has the owners' bulletin, certificates for which weeks I've reserved and the most recent catalog of exchanges.

Writing

My writing files take up an entire file drawer and would not be needed by most couples.

How Long?

Once you've set up a filing system and are keeping good records, you'll probably wonder how long to keep those records. Most of us are somewhere between "throw it all away" and "hoarder."

You don't want to toss something important and soon find that you need it and have to get a duplicate somehow. On the other hand, you don't want to live in a hazardous environment, surrounded by bulging boxes of yellowing papers.

The records most people are concerned with keeping are tax returns, bank statements, brokerage statements, charge account bills and medical information—in other words, papers that could identify us to thieves.

So, do you toss or keep the following papers?

Tax Records

The IRS says it's okay to throw out tax records after three years, seven if you're suspected of fraud. If you are a fraud suspect, you have more problems than deciding how long to keep records.

I was audited because my tax preparer listed the total amount of my stock sales as profit, which would have meant a huge tax bill, plus penalty. Because Tom had kept good records, I was able to find proof of the purchase price for all but one stock, which we'd owned for more than three years.

Marty Hines had an unsettling experience with the IRS after her husband's death. "I got a notice one day that there was a refund due but our tax return had not been filed and the three-year period for claiming the refund would be up the next week. I panicked. The tax partner at our firm told me he knew what Anthony had been doing. He'd figure the returns each year up to the point that he knew we'd get a refund and wouldn't be penalized for late filing, then turn to his clients' work. He'd do this for three years, then file all three at the same time.

"Unfortunately, he got sick the year he was to file and didn't get it done. If I hadn't gotten that card and followed up on it, I'd have lost a lot of money. As it was, I spent every night for a week getting all the papers together for the tax preparer, then filed the state and federal returns in person, and got the refunds. In going through the tax papers, I found a bundle of notices from the IRS reminding him that our returns were overdue, which he'd hidden from me."

Marty, understandably, urges all spouses to be knowledgeable about the family finances and recordkeeping.

Bank Statements

Statements should be checked the day they arrive by mail, or several times a week online, to make sure there are no unauthorized charges and that checks have cleared. If the checkbook and the statement are in sync, keep the statements for only three months. If there are tax deductible items paid by check, save the printout that shows the miniature photo of your check. (Old advice to "save canceled checks" is useless today; no one gets them.)

ATM slips

Keep them only until the bank statement arrives, then shred them.

Brokerage Statements

Stockbrokers are now required to send a yearly statement showing purchases, sales, profit and loss. This statement is labeled "1099 Consolidated." When this arrives, it's safe to shred the monthly statements. If you receive statements online, you'll want to print out a copy of the 1099 Consolidated for the tax preparer and one for yourself. Keep these statements as long as you own the stocks listed on the statement or you have a loss carry-forward.

Utility Bills

These should be kept for only three months. Ditto for charge account statements, unless there are tax-deductible items charged. Then circle the listing, staple your receipt to the statement and place it in your Taxes file.

Home Insurance Policies

Keep these for a minimum of five years, but 10 is better.

Home Repair Bills

Keep for 10 years to protect you in case of a dispute about the work. If there is a lien related to the repairs, make sure you get a statement of satisfaction from the contractor and keep it as long as you own the property.

Life Insurance Policies

Keep these as long as you have coverage, or until it is redeemed or canceled, then for three additional years.

Pay Stubs

Keep individual ones until your end-of-year summary arrives, then shred all but the summary.

Medical Records

Keep for five years after treatment has ended, unless you deducted medical expenses on your taxes. In that case, keep them for seven years.

Mortgage Documents

Keep the mortgage documents until you have paid off the mortgage. Then obtain proof of satisfaction from the mortgage lender, and keep it as long as you own the property. (Be sure to notify your insurance carrier that your loan has been paid off.)

> **1** Like closets and other storage areas, your files should be examined at least yearly, perhaps at the beginning of the new year when end-of-year statements arrive.

You may find that you can consolidate some files, toss out others altogether, or expand categories to include more possibilities. In any case, a good filing system will save you time and money, and your survivors will be very grateful.

Checklist for Chapter 10

- ☐ Get a place to put all your papers.
- ☐ Get your filing supplies.
- ☐ Gather all your papers together.
- ☐ Clear out some space to work.
- ☐ Dedicate time for filing.
- ☐ Toss out anything you don't need.
- ☐ Examine your files at least once per year, consolidating, expanding or tossing out files as appropriate.

CHAPTER 11
MAKING A LIST, CHECKING IT TWICE

Lists are everywhere: The 10 Most Beautiful Women, 12 Cleaning Tips, 4 Ways to Lose Belly Fat , 7 Things Men/Women Hate on a Date, Top 10 Movies, etc. Most such lists don't affect your life, but some lists can be very important to you.

Maybe you have personal lists in your purse, beside the phone or on your iPad: lists of chores you need to get done today, a few friends' phone numbers, items to shop for. Most of us have such lists.

But what if you died suddenly? What kind of lists would your survivors need? Here are a few suggestions for some of these lists.

Create a new section in your notebook labeled In Case of Emergency; these lists will be filed there.

It's also a good idea to keep your lists on a flash drive, in case you have to flee in an emergency. You won't have time to grab assorted folders, notebooks or loose sheets of paper.

Whom to Notify

The first list survivors need after a death or accident is the names of people they should notify, including family members, employers and close friends. This may seem foolish. Surely you know your family's contact information. But a stranger—a nurse, doctor or emergency personnel—may be making the call. Both of you may be in an accident and be incapacitated. Or you may be so numb with shock that you can't remember vital everyday things.

 Start with your immediate family, giving contact information (first and last name, relationship, phone number, email address and postal address).

Next on your list should be employers and/or supervisors, with name, position and contact information.

After this come your more far-reaching contacts. For me, this means cousins on both sides of the family, some with notations about the groups they will then contact, friends, my priest, financial advisor, my editor if I am working on a book, a writer friend with the notation "To notify writers group" and the newsletter editor of a group I am close to, Teachers for East Africa.

In addition to a lengthy contact list in my file, I also carry a card in my purse, headed "In Case of Emergency, Please Notify." It contains the names and phone numbers of my daughter, sister and a close friend. These numbers are also programmed into my cell phone.

Medical Information

Medical histories and medicines taken should be next on your list. Whenever you're checking in at a doctor's office or hospital, you'll be asked questions that need exact answers. Can you remember the names of all the medicines you're taking and what the doses are and how often they are taken? Do you recall the dates of all your surgeries? The dates and causes of death of family members? Most of us don't. So check, and write it all down.

 Make a separate sheet for each family member outlining all this vital information, and save a copy on your flash drive.

 Update this information regularly, deleting medicines you are no longer taking, and making whatever additions are necessary.

This list may save you from bad reactions to medications, or even sudden death.

Numbers

 List the names of your banks, the type of account(s) you have and the account numbers.

These numbers appear on your bank statements, but it is handy to have them all in one place, especially when only one of you is the financial partner.

Marty Hines, an estates and trusts paralegal, said, "You wouldn't believe how many widows I dealt with who had no idea what bills the family owed, what insurance they had or even what bank accounts existed. I had to resort to emailing all the local banks in the area on a couple of occasions."

 For online bank accounts, add the password.

A friend, Bill, told me that after his wife died, he began closing accounts in her name and consolidating others. She had handled all the banking online, right up to her last stay in the hospital, but had not written down the passwords. One account is still inaccessible, since he doesn't know the password.

Your survivors may be able to gain access to accounts by writing the company and sending a death certificate, but it is a tedious process. It's much more sensible to furnish your spouse and heirs with passwords.

Bill also recommends a special email account for financial matters. It should not be tied to an employer, which may cease quickly after a death or job change. And it should not be an account that will be canceled if it is not logged onto regularly.

He suggests an alumni account: "Most universities make a permanent email address available to alums, even those who have not graduated, in the hopes of eventual donations. Use it, along with an ID and password and an email forwarder, which can be used to forward email to another account. All my financial email comes to my own personal account, and I do not have multiple email accounts to look at every day. Then, if my brother has to disentangle my finances after I'm gone, he can have the financial emails redirected to his account."

Other numbers that you should list are for frequent flyer accounts as well as other associations, such as timeshares and hotel affinity accounts. Those miles or points will be lost to you without the membership number and PIN or password.

For credit cards and ATM cards, you'll also need to list the card numbers as well as the PIN, and—in case your card is lost or stolen—the contact number to call, which is listed on the back of the card.

Some advisors suggest photocopying the front and back of all your cards as well as your passport; take a copy with you when you travel and leave a copy with a trusted friend or relative. This makes it possible to quickly report their loss or theft and get replacements.

Passwords

If you have passwords for other accounts, write them down. Otherwise, you may not be able to open your email, trade stocks online, refill medicine prescriptions or access information you have paid for. I still have many of my passwords on a Rolodex file, under the name of the company, such as D for Delta Airlines.

 It is especially important to write down the passwords if you change them often as you are advised to do. Only a genius could remember a dozen passwords, often with small variations. After a few unsuccessful attempts, you will be locked out of accessing that account for that day.

Family Information

List each family member's birthday, anniversaries and other significant information.

Whichever of you survives may need this to continue commemorating special family occasions. It can be in a list arranged by dates or arranged alphabetically. Or the data can be recorded on a giant calendar, with a column for each month.

Sample Family Information List

Legal name: Spouse's name:

Date of birth:

Social Security #

My will was written (updated) on: It's located at:

My executors are:

Addresses & phone #s

My attorney is:
    Address and phone #s

My doctor is:

My employer is:

My bank accounts _____ & _____ are at _____ Bank,
    Address & phone #

Safe deposit box, # _____ is at _____ Bank.   Its key is at:

My broker is: My account # is:

I am a citizen of :   My blood type is:

My passport # is: It expires on:

My driver's license # is:

My nearest of kin is: Address & phone #

My children: Dates of birth

Father: Mother:

Other relatives:

Pets:

Education: List schools attended, dates, and degrees (if any)

Memberships:

Church: Name, address & phone #; name of priest (pastor, rabbi)

Other Memberships: If an officer in an organization, where are the
    records?

Military Service: Dates, rank, termination?

Helpers

This list will include doctors, dentists, vets, grooming services, attorneys, hairdressers, plumbers, electricians, landscapers and other people whose services you employ.

List each helper's name, their specialty or occupation, telephone number and the date that person's services were last used.

I admit that I rely mainly on business cards stapled to the Rolodex cards, with the carpet cleaning service under C and the handyman who cleans gutters under H. I'm trying to improve by following my own advice. If I'd noted the date of my last physical, with my family doctor, I wouldn't have let two years elapse between checkups.

Where Things Are

This may be your most important list. It doesn't matter what records you keep or what objects you own, if you can't find them. You need to keep track of your property. Every dry cleaner has unclaimed clothing that someone brought in but forgot to come for (or perhaps the owner died or moved away). Most states occasionally hold auctions of unclaimed property. Don't let your belongings end up as salvage.

List all of your belongings that are not currently in your possession or that aren't in logical, clearly labeled places. This list should probably be arranged by objects, but should also include a date as well as a destination. For example, "Winter coats taken to Miller's for cleaning and storage, May 18." "Will in bottom left drawer of file cabinet, revised 3/12/2010." "Old tax returns in box in garage."

 Update your list as items are moved: the stored clothing collected, the lawn mower left for repair picked up, some items given away or discarded, etc.

I admit to almost losing a favorite pair of shoes. I left them for new heel taps to be added and was told the repairman was ill and there was a backup of repairs, possibly a couple of months. One day I looked through my closet for shoes and remembered the repair shop. A "Where is it" notation would have saved me time searching. Fortunately the shop keeps better records than I do, and found my shoes—still unrepaired, but they soon will be.

 Also list any item you lend someone else—that is, if you hope to get it back.

Tom had both a student violin and an adult sized, and loaned the student instrument to a choir member whose son wanted to study violin. We moved and forgot the instrument—until our daughter wanted to study violin. We wrote the borrowers, who sent us a violin, but not Tom's. They'd forgotten where they got the violin and when their son lost interest, they gave it away. They had to go out and buy a used one to send us.

It was too big for Catherine, who needed a half size, but a visiting friend said she'd like to borrow it and reclaim the musical skill she'd once had. We let her have it and promptly forgot that she was the borrower. Catherine by now was ready for the full-size violin, but who had it? Not until we were packing to move did Shirley appear with the violin, to our relief. We eventually sold it at a yard sale. Easy come, easy go, especially if you don't write down where your property is and who has it.

Checklist for Chapter 11

☐ Create a new section in your notebook labeled In Case of Emergency for these lists.

Whom to Notify:

☐ List the first and last name, relationship, phone number, email address and postal address of your immediate family members, followed by employers and/or supervisors, extended family members, friends and contact points for organizations you belong to.

☐ Consider carrying a card in your walled labeled "In Case of Emergency," listing the names and phone numbers of three close relatives and/or friends to contact.

Medical Information:

☐ Make a separate sheet for each family member outlining all their medical information, including medication names and dosages, dates of all surgeries and dates and causes of death of family members.

☐ Update medical information regularly, deleting medicines that are no loner being taken, and making whatever additions are necessary.

Numbers:

☐ List the names of your banks, the type of account(s) you have and the account numbers.

☐ For online bank accounts, add the password.

☐ For credit cards and ATM cards, list the card numbers, the PIN, and the contact number to call in case your card is lost or stolen.

Passwords:

☐ List passwords for any other accounts.

☐ Update all passwords as they are changed.

Family Information:

☐ List each family member's birthday, anniversaries and other significant information.

Helpers:

☐ List all of the doctors, dentists, vets, grooming services, attorneys, hairdressers, plumbers, electricians, landscapers and other people whose services you employ. List each helper's name, their specialty or occupation, telephone number and the date that person's services were last used.

Where Things Are:

☐ List all of your belongings that are not currently in your possession or that aren't in logical, clearly labeled places. Include the date you last had the item.

☐ Update your list as items are moved.

CHAPTER 12
REMEMBERING YOU

What do you want people to read about you after you're gone?

When a famous person dies, his or her obituary and life story immediately appear in great detail in all the media, along with photos of the celebrity in various places and situations. If the deceased appeared in films, clips will be shown on TV. The facts were gathered, the tone established and the story written and periodically updated well before the celebrity's death.

Even though you may not be famous, you owe it to yourself and your loved ones to write your own obituary so that you may be remembered in the way you wish to be. Your survivors may be too distraught at the time of your death to recall all the information you would want included, and your adult children may not know much about your youth. . If this is not your first marriage, would your present spouse know enough about your early life to write your obituary in an appropriate manner?

If you haven't written your own obituary, your bereaved family may simply be asked a few brief questions about you and the actual writing of the obituary is done by the funeral home or cremation society. Do you want the final summing up of your life left to a stranger?

Writing your own obituary is difficult. Many people avoid

this because it means facing your own mortality. However, summing up your life in writing will benefit your survivors, and it might bring up some interesting topics of discussion between you and your family. It's a popular assignment in creative writing classes and in counseling sessions to inspire the writers to look ahead and express what they hope to accomplish, so it's not necessarily an intimation of death.

Andrew, whose wife died after a long fight against cancer, said, "Her death wasn't sudden and I knew I'd have to write her obituary, but we couldn't bring ourselves to talk about it. I found it very stressful after her death to write her obituary, and I had to call her sister out of state to help me with details. I almost omitted her only surviving aunt. If Katie had written it herself, it would have been a more complete document of her life, and I would have had the satisfaction of knowing it was exactly what she wanted."

How long do you want your obituary to be? What would you be willing to pay for its publication, or for your family to pay? Some newspapers will insert a simple death notice furnished by the funeral home, stating name, date of death, city and funeral arrangements, free of charge. There may be a charge for a longer, more detailed obituary, and in some cases this can run to hundreds of dollars. The choice of what and how much to say in your obituary is yours.

Writing your Obituary

 Begin with your formal name, followed by a nickname you're well known by, if any. Anyone who has changed a name should note both previous and present names. Married women should indicate first names, maiden name and married last name.

Obituaries

Donald Gladieux

Donald Clement Gladieux, 85, of Hendersonville, a local business leader and outstanding animal rights advocate, died at his home on June 5, 2009.

Donald Gladieux was born in Fort Wayne, Ind., on Jan. 14, 1924, to the late Veronica Pepe and Clem Gladieux. After earning a Purple Heart as an Army paratrooper in the Pacific during World War II, he attended college on the G.I. Bill and joined the Kimberly-Clark Corp. as a human resources manager (then called "personnel manager"). He was promoted to plant manager for the company, first in Wisconsin, then in Tennessee, and finally in Hendersonville at Berkeley Mills, which he managed from 1972 until 1981.

He lost his mother to tuberculosis while he was just a toddler and was raised partly by his maternal grandparents on their farm. When his father remarried, he returned to Fort Wayne, where he attended Catholic schools until he was old enough to contribute to the family income.

Gladieux

Still a teenager, he worked as a service station attendant, stockroom clerk and assembler on a production line manufacturing motors for General Electric.

He went into service in February 1943 and volunteered for the Army paratroops. He was assigned to F Company, 511th Parachute Infantry Regiment of the 11th Airborne Division, which was headquartered at Camp Mackall near Ft. Bragg. Jump school was at Ft. Benning in Georgia; the unit also trained at Camp Polk, La., before departing for the Asiatic-Pacific Theatre in May 1944.

As a paratroop rifleman, he took part in the Battle of Leyte and the Battle of Luzon before being wounded by enemy fire in an assault on Manila in the Philippines. He was awarded an Asiatic-Pacific Theatre Ribbon with three battle stars, a Philippine Liberation Ribbon with one star, a Good Conduct medal and a Purple Heart.

He returned home to marry Rose Marie Shattuck, also a native of Fort Wayne, with whom he had corresponded throughout the war. Despite not having finished 10th grade, his test scores qualified him for admission to Indiana University, where he completed his A.B. degree in 1951 and an M.B.A. in 1953. He was recruited by Kimberly-Clark and joined the company as personnel manager for a plant in Menasha, Wis.

In the 1960s, he achieved notable success negotiating labor contracts with the Teamsters at Kimberly-Clark's plant in Niagara Falls. He became known within the company as a tough-minded troubleshooter and turnaround agent. When he was sent to Hendersonville's Berkeley Mills plant in 1972, his assignment was to get its affairs in order and close it down. But finding the town and people of Hendersonville very appealing, he decided to attempt to redeem Berkeley Mills and keep it open. His efforts were successful, and the plant remains in operation today.

Upon taking early retirement from Kimberly-Clark in order to remain in Hendersonville, he became an investment adviser. He and Rose Marie founded Investment Planners International in partnership with Howard Smith. Other ventures included buying and rehabilitating the former Belk Simpson building on Main Street. He and Rose Marie also purchased and managed the General Travel Agency, building new offices at 117 West Barnwell St.

He, Rose Marie and their three daughters lived in the Tranquility development in Flat Rock, and it was here that he befriended a neighbor's cow and decided to save it from slaughter. The story found its way into the Hendersonville Times-News and resulted in him receiving distress calls whenever an animal was found abandoned or injured at a roadside. He and Rose Marie took up the cause of animal welfare in Henderson County and founded the Animal Welfare Alliance, a 501(c)(3) foundation whose mission was to try to persuade various local animal welfare organizations to work together more effectively. The Animal Welfare Alliance has also underwritten free spay/neutering campaigns in cooperation with several area veterinary clinics.

He was a major contributor to All Creatures Great and Small, a no-kill animal shelter whose facility was unfortunately overcrowded and under-financed. In an unofficial capacity, he labored to rectify the shelter's standing in the community and with authorities in Raleigh so that its hundreds of resident animals would not have to be destroyed. His efforts were partially successful, buying time so that many of the animals could be adopted or transferred to other shelters before All Creatures closed in 2008.

He was a lifelong Catholic whose differences with certain church policies didn't undermine his faith. He and Rose Marie once spent a summer volunteering at a Boy Scout camp. He served on several state and regional business advisory boards. He was a Patron of Quality at Western Carolina University and an honorary Kentucky Colonel.

He was a beloved husband, father and grandfather. He is survived by Rose Marie, his wife of 62 years; his daughter, Deni, and her husband, Will McIntyre, of Winston-Salem; daughter Lynn and her husband, Steve Hamilton, of the Woodlands, Texas; and daughter Cheryl and her husband, Ron Allari, of Alexandria, Ky. He is survived by three grandchildren, Jennifer Powell, Emily Pow-

Obituaries can be brief or very, very long
Reprinted from the Times-News, *Hendersonville, NC*

Since you probably don't know the age at which you'll die, you'll want to leave the age blank. It can be filled in at the appropriate time.

 Next come your city and state of residence.

For security and identify theft reasons, it's not a good idea to mention your exact date of birth or your exact street address. Clever thieves have been known to rob the home while mourners are at a funeral. (More on guarding against this will appear in a chapter in Part II.)

I made two mistakes in writing Tom's obituary. First, I stated when and where he had been born and gave his parents' full names. An identity thief could have used that information, but as far as I know,

Lilian J. Braun, 97

Braun

TRYON — Lilian Jackson Braun Bettinger, 97, a prolific best-selling author of The Cat Who mystery series for more than 40 years, died of natural causes Saturday, June 4, 2011, at Hospice House of the Carolina Foothills in Landrum, S.C., June 4, 2011. She had lived in Tryon for the past 23 years.

She wrote 31 books (2 collections of short stories and 29 the Cat Who books).

Dutton published her first book, The Cat Who Could Read Backwards, in 1966. The New York Times labeled her "the new detective of the year". Two more followed with critical acclaim (The Cat Who Ate Danish Modern and The Cat Who Turned On and Off). There was an 18-year hiatus between the third and fourth books.

The Cat Who novels, considered light, humorous mysteries, have been translated into 16 languages, distributed worldwide, and sold in the millions. Her books were standards on the New York Times best seller list. Beginning in 1990, her books reached the prestigious list for 20 consecutive years.

She wrote all of her books in long hand. They were published with limited editing. "I don't pay attention to the publishing business. I just write my kitty-cat stories."

Braun (who once wrote "A dog has his day, but cats have 365") retired from writing in 2007 after the publication of The Cat Who Had 60 Whiskers.

Writing was a lifelong passion. "I always wrote,

a copywriter and ending as the director of public relations. She took time off to write her first three books and then accepted a position as the "The Good Living" editor for the Detroit Free Press. She wrote feature articles on interior design, art and architecture, as well as reviews of kitchen gadgets and other household products. She remained with the Detroit Free Press for 30 years.

Lilian Jackson Braun Bettinger was born on June 20, 1913, in Willimansette, Chicopee Falls, Mass. Her father, Charles Jackson, was an inventor and industrial manufacturing troubleshooter. Her mother, Clara Ward Jackson, was a homemaker. Her father's work took them to Rhode Island, Brooklyn, N.Y. and to Detroit, Mich. She lived in Michigan until she retired to North Carolina.

In 2005, the Polk County Public Library in Columbus held a tribute to Lilian Jackson Braun for her lifetime achievement and community involvement. It was an evening of song, limericks, readings and tributes. Braun served as the honorary writer in residence for the library as well as honorary chairperson of the 2005 library card sign-up campaign, where she created the tag line, "A library card is the beginning of a lifelong adventure".

She was preceded in death by husband, Louis Paul Braun; a sister, Florence Jackson, and a brother, Lloyd Jackson.

She is survived by her husband of 32 years, Earl Bettinger.

No memorial services will be held.

Donations may be made to Hospice House of the Carolina Foothills, 260 Fairwinds Road, Landrum, S.C. 29356.

Condolences may be sent to www.pettyfuneralhome.com.

Petty Funeral Home and Crematory, Landrum, S.C.

Reprinted from the Times-News, *Hendersonville, NC*

no harm has come from my mistake. (I realized the error almost immediately and took steps to make sure no one got credit in his name, which I'll discuss in Chapter 17.)

Second, I did not say, "of Portsmouth." The death certificate gave his address, the memorial service was held in a Portsmouth church, and it was noted that he was survived by me, "of Portsmouth." However, none of that appeared in the first line of the obituary, which was sent to the regional newspaper by the cremation society, headquartered in Virginia Beach, twenty miles from our home. The newspaper covers a large area and publishes obituaries by the city in which the deceased lived. Hence, Tom's obituary appeared in the listing for Virginia Beach, and was overlooked by friends and neighbors who read only the obituaries from their own cities.

 Choose the term you prefer to describe your death.

"Died" is the most commonly used in obituaries, but you may prefer "passed away," "died in his sleep," "died suddenly (tragically)" or a more religious statement such as "entered eternal life," followed by the date of death. The date of your death should obviously be left blank for now. Someone else can fill it in at the proper time.

 Let your survivors know if you wish to have your cause of death noted.

You probably don't know now what you will die of and you may consider it a personal matter not meant for publication. Some general explanations often used in obituaries are "after a long illness," "from a heart attack," "following an automobile accident" and "of age-related causes."

Here's an example of the opening statement of an obituary: "John ('Jack') Carlyle Smith, 89, of Chicago, died April 5, -- in Mercy Hospital of age related causes."

C-2 The News & Advance, Lynchburg, Va., Tuesday, February 3, 2004

Edna Lollis Thomas

Edna Lollis Thomas died of old age on Jan. 29, 2004. Despite 65 years of immoderate smoking, she reached the age of 88. Adopting this behavior as a role model is not recommended. She had two daughters, one of whom died at the age of 16. She would have been of greater comfort and joy to her throughout her life than the other, but the surviving one did the best she could and will miss her. To her, Edna gave the gift of music by introducing her to classical music via Jose Iturbi movies when she was but a child and by bequeathing to her the ability to play by ear. After hearing her piano teacher play, Edna could reproduce the piece, only pretending to look at the notes, the necessity of which she never acknowledged. She played the piano to the end of her life, even after having one hand slightly affected by a stroke. Fate was kind in its choice of afflictions. Her macular degeneration, while making her almost blind, did not affect her musical ear. She also adjusted to this handicap with humor. Once her husband Albert, in a vain attempt to convince her that she could not see well enough to continue driving, admonished her. "Edna, you know you didn't see that sign at the gas station the other day!" She replied: "That's absolutely not true. I didn't see the gas station!"

Being the daughter of a minister and having been forced to attend church regularly as a child, her repertoire of the hymns she could reproduce on the piano was almost unlimited. Her church-going did not extend into her old age, but this did not stop her from living a true Christian life which could serve as an example to many of those who never miss a Sunday. As for the short time after Albert died, she and a friend took advantage of the handicap permit in his name hanging on the rear view mirror to find good parking spaces for their shopping trips. Once she speculated about what she would say, if anyone, upon seeing two ladies get into the car, should ask: "Where is Albert?" She concluded that she would answer: "That's a good question. Where IS he?"

Perhaps because of her sense of humor and positive outlook, Edna made friends easily. Despite moving to Lynchburg late in life, at the age of 73, she quickly found a circle of friends. Every Saturday some of them gathered at her house for Happy Hour(s). The last one, which was less than a week before her death, lasted for three hours and still when it came time to go, she begged everyone, as usual, to stay a bit longer. Often, these occasions included piano playing and talk of politics. Her political views could best be described as "compromise rather than fight." Her solution to the race to space between the Soviet Union and the United States was "let them take the moon and we'll take the sun." Her approach to health defied logic but seemed to work for her. Maintaining that smoking protected her from germs was but one aspect. After her stroke, she was given a small squeeze ball to strengthen the affected right hand. Asked by her daughter why she was exercising her left hand instead, she replied, with her own brand of logic, that the exercise was much easier with the left hand. The right hand got better anyway.

Thoughtful, even concerning her death, she donated her body for medical research. If there is a hereafter she is no doubt urging all of us from there to do the same. Aside from the humanitarian motivation, she didn't want her daughter to be burdened with excessive funeral bills. Should anyone be moved to make a monetary contribution in her memory, speculating on future savings from funerals or for other reasons, please send donations to the Lynchburg Humane Society, 3305 Naval Reserve Road, Lynchburg, from which her daughter adopted Edna's adored "grand-dog" Josh. He is also grieving her death, but will soon benefit from her death by a needed weight loss caused by the absence of his ever dependable, incurable violator of all rules against feeding dogs unhealthy human tidbits from the table and elsewhere.

There will be a memorial happy hour to celebrate the life of Edna Lollis Thomas for happy hour regulars and other friends and family on Feb. 7, 2004.

---

out, all the essential elements are included in this unconventional obituary. Read on to see why readers of Lynchburg's *The News & Advance* are looking forward to the next installment of the Edna Thomas series, "Edna's Funeral Goes on the Road". Don't you wish you had known Edna?!

This letter to the editor from Linda Thomas, daughter of Edna and writer of the obituary, indicates the positive response she received.

Celebration of life

I would like to express my gratitude to all who responded, both directly to me and indirectly through The News & Advance, to the obituary honoring my mother Edna Lollis Thomas. I am especially grateful to Darrell Laurant for his excellent column.

It is a tribute to my mother that her "insignificant" life touched so many strangers and made them and those who knew her able to laugh — even upon the occasion of her death. The memorial happy hour was a true celebration of her life. The mood continued into the next morning at breakfast with two relatives and my closest friend.

It was suggested that I go ahead and buy the small camper I have been wanting with the money saved from not having a funeral. It would be named "Edna's Funeral" and there would be a follow-up to the obituary called "Edna's Funeral Goes on the Road." No doubt some will find this morbid and disrespectful, but my mother would love it. After all, it was not her death that made us laugh, but her life and, fortunately, that spirit of craziness lives on in us.

LINDA THOMAS
Lynchburg

Obituaries can even be light-hearted and fun.
Reprinted from the News & Advance, *Lynchburg, VA*

Then list the names of your survivors: spouse, children, grandchildren, parents, siblings, nieces, nephews, aunts and uncles.

For example: "She was the daughter of the late Samuel and Ann Johnson, and is survived by her husband, Andrew Smith, two sons, …, etc. " Their places of residence may be mentioned, such as "A daughter, Ann Smith, of Chicago." Deceased immediate relatives and spouses should be named and noted, as for example, "He was preceded in death by a brother, Frank Smith." Or, "He was previously married to the late Mary Smith."

 Next, list high school attended, colleges attended and degrees earned.

 Your occupation and possible military service come next, followed by organizations you belong to, honors won, significant publications and special interests or hobbies you wish mentioned.

For example, "Louis served in the U. S. Army, rising to the rank of Captain. After his return to civilian life, he worked as an engineer for Kimberly Paper Company in ---. He was twice chosen Employee of the Month. He was the author of several books on management. (Name them) After his retirement, he took up gardening and became a Master Gardener."

 Mention religious affiliation, if any, and positions held within that group, as "He was an elder in the ---church where he had been a member for 30 years."

 If you wish to be remembered for some special qualities, such as wit, generosity or enthusiasm for life, say so.

This is your last chance to represent yourself to the world.

For example, "Mary was known throughout the area for her excellent cooking, and she won awards for her cakes. She was generous in sharing her know-how and her recipes with friends."

 If you have lived for some length of time in other places, mention those places. Note at the beginning or end of your obituary that it is to be sent to newspapers in those places. (Give the name and address of out-of-town newspapers.) Notices of your death should also be sent to your college alumni associations and any professional or trade groups to which you belong.

 Mention charities you would like remembered. For example, "In lieu of flowers, contributions may be sent to the Salvation Army." A website may be listed for distant friends to express condolences.

Do you want a service held in your memory? Our next chapter will deal with planning such a service, and your survivors will need to add the time and place of this service to your obituary, or to indicate if it is private, such as "A private memorial service will be held at a later date." If none is to be held, that should be noted.

 Say whether there will be visitation, either at the home of the deceased or at a funeral home.

 Do you want a photo to accompany your obituary? If so, do you want a recent photo or an earlier favorite one? Keep the photo with your obituary.

 Both spouses should write their obituaries and should read each other's.

 Reread and update them once a year.

My mother had written her obituary, and we four children

were relieved that none of us had to write it. She knew names and dates that we might not have known or might have overlooked mentioning.

If either of you have published or achieved something else that would cause you to be listed on Google, Yahoo or other search engines, your obituary will also be indexed there, so consider carefully how you wish to be remembered.

 After you complete your obituary, place it in your "In the Event of My Death" file (see Chapter 10, Keeping Tabs).

Checklist for Chapter 12

☐ Begin with your formal name, followed by a nickname you're well known by, if any.

☐ Leave your age blank.

☐ List your city and state of residence.

☐ Choose the term you prefer to describe your death.

☐ Let your survivors know if you wish to have your cause of death noted.

☐ List the names of your survivors: spouse, children, grandchildren, parents, siblings, nieces, nephews, aunts and uncles.

☐ List high school attended, colleges attended and degrees earned.

☐ List your occupation and possible military service, followed by organizations you belong to, honors won, significant publications and special interests or hobbies you wish mentioned.

☐ Mention your religious affiliation, if any, and positions held within that group.

☐ If you wish to be remembered for some special qualities, such as wit, generosity or enthusiasm for life, say so.

☐ If you have lived for some length of time in other places, list those places and note at the beginning or end of your obituary that it is to be sent to newspapers in those places. (Give the name and address of out-of-town newspapers.)

☐ Mention charities you would like remembered.

☐ Say whether there will be visitation, either at the home of the deceased or at a funeral home.

☐ Both spouses should write their obituaries and should read each other's.

☐ Reread and update your obituaries once a year.

☐ After you complete your obituary, place it in your "In the Event of My Death" file.

CHAPTER 13
IT'S YOUR FUNERAL

The expression "It's your funeral" is usually meant as a warning that you're about to do something that may turn out badly. Here, I'm using it to mean that you can plan your own funeral, as elaborate or simple as you wish, within reason. You can go out in style, if you're willing and able to pay for it up front.

Unless you're a head of state, you won't qualify for the kind of daylong extravaganza of the funeral of former President Ronald Reagan or the weeklong memorial for the Princess of Wales, replete with attending royalty, military escorts, high security, 21-gun salutes and Air Force flyover. Most of us wouldn't qualify for—or want—such treatment of our earthly remains.

Perhaps you want a lively procession and a big party afterward for friends and family. You could opt for a somber service with bagpiper. Or you could choose to have no service at all. After all, it's your funeral.

Whichever category you fall in, give some thought now to your funeral and make your wishes known to your family, in writing. Your survivors should feel confident that they are following your wishes and can disregard critics who opine, "That's not what he would have wanted," or "It's a pity to spend so much on a funeral. It doesn't help anybody."

Funeral practices have varied through the centuries among

different cultures. Some seem to us gruesome, such as putting the body out for ravens to pick clean before its burial. Some deceased were pushed out from shore on a burning barge, or burned on a pyre. Others were committed to a river or an ice floe. On the American frontier, friends and relatives of the deceased bathed and dressed the body before it was buried, and a formal religious service might be held months later when a minister made his rounds of the settlements. The use of funeral directors is a fairly recent development, but one that most Americans choose.

What Do You Want?

Do you want a private funeral, with only immediate family members present, or a very public one, open to all who hear of your death or read your obituary? Will it be religious, secular or military, or a combination? Do you want to be cremated, or embalmed and buried in a casket with a protective vault? Or do you want your body donated to a medical school so that future doctors may learn from you? By making your wishes clear, you will spare your survivor being pressured into making an emotional decision or perhaps buying a more expensive and less satisfying funeral than you would have wished.

 Examine your options, considering the laws of your state and the availability of facilities near you.

Cremation

My husband Tom was cremated, by his prior stated wishes, as were my sister and several friends, and I'm choosing cremation for myself. It is the simplest and least expensive of options. At present about 35 percent of bodies in the United States are cremated, and it is estimated that the figure will rise to 59 percent by 2025.

In some states, if the deceased is cremated within 24 hours of death, there is no requirement for embalming. If, however, you wish to have a "viewing" or "visitation," for which the body will need to be preserved for several days, then embalming is necessary. Once cremation has been done, the service can be held whenever it is convenient for survivors. The ashes, or "cremains," can be scattered at some place that is meaningful to you, buried in a family plot, stored in an urn or divided into smaller urns so that several people can have a part of you.

About the only downside is that some religions oppose cremation. If cremation is your first choice, discuss this with your spiritual adviser.

Donation

If you choose to donate your body for medical research, the remains will probably be cremated afterward and the cremains returned to your family for disposition.

 If you do plan to have all or part of your body donated, make those arrangements now.

Contact the director of a nearby teaching hospital or medical society and discuss your options. One such medical school is at Ohio State University. The school arranges a special memorial service for donors of bodies.

Burial

If you choose burial, where do you want it to be?

 Choose a site and buy a burial plot, preferably in an established cemetery that has ongoing upkeep.

When Gail's husband was in intensive care and his doctors told her he had only hours to live, she and her son visited a cemetery, chose a plot and made funeral arrangements. He lived for several more months, but Gail said choosing ahead of time made the trauma of his death easier to bear.

What type of coffin do you want? If you choose burial, you (or your heirs) will be required to buy a cement vault as well. This is not to keep the body from deteriorating—it will anyway—but to keep the earth from sinking in your grave as the coffin decays.

What clothing do you wish to be buried in?

 Put your chosen clothing in a place where it can be found, with a label indicating its purpose.

What music do you want? What kind of flowers? Do you want your own poetry or a letter to be read at your funeral? Do you plan to videotape yourself saying goodbye and have it played during the service? (This taping could also be a supplement to your will, to assure your heirs that at the time of preparing the will you were "of sound mind.")

Paying for a Burial

Many people who plan to be buried discuss their plans with a funeral director and even pay in advance for the funeral, so they will know that this matter is taken care of and that they need not provide for payment of it in a will. (Never include funeral instructions in your will, as it will very likely not be read until after your funeral.)

Prepaying for a funeral can be risky, so be sure to do your research.

 Go online to www.funerals.org to learn more about prices and options. Be sure to ask the funeral director how your funds will be handled and what would happen if the funeral home went out of business or if you moved elsewhere and wanted to transfer. Could you change your mind about the details, or even cancel the service?

It's recommended that you put the money for your prepaid service in a "Totten trust" account, which can be opened at any bank. The amount will be paid out to your survivors or your executor at your death. John Hundley noted that if you prepay your funeral, the money is put into escrow and you will earn interest, which must be reported as taxable income.

Viewing

Do you want your remains to be viewed? It will be the last memory some people will have of you. Will it be a pleasant one? Sometimes the mortician can smooth out wrinkles and remove pain lines so that the deceased looks "natural" or even better than in his/her last days. However, if the deceased has been horribly disfigured by an accident or fire, or has been ravaged by a lengthy illness, a closed coffin visitation, with perhaps a good photo displayed, would be better.

 Make your wishes regarding a viewing known, subject to change by your survivors if circumstances indicate.

Your Memorial Service

There are many ways to commemorate a life. It's up to you to choose how you wish to be commemorated.

 Decide what you want for your final ceremony, put it in writing, and place it in your file "In the Event of My Death."

My British friend Margaret belonged to no church and had made her after-death wishes known. Her service was held at the crematorium, and the bulletin distributed to mourners had photos of Margaret riding an elephant in Thailand, and of Margaret curtsying to Princess Anne when the Princess visited the school in Doha, Qatar, where Margaret was teaching. Several poems were read at the service, which concluded with a recording of Frank Sinatra singing "I Did It My Way." She had planned her funeral her way.

Andrew's wife had chosen several poems and spiritual readings she wanted read at her funeral. She had also chosen taped music that she especially liked, though it was not Andrew's favorite, but he followed her wishes.

I chose for Tom a traditional Episcopalian service, with the congregation singing four of his favorite hymns. The only flowers were white orchids on the altar and several arrangements that friends had sent. Since no body was present, Catherine and I, at the minister's suggestion, chose objects that represented his life: his favorite hat and bowtie, his violin, his lacrosse letter sweater from college, a small toolbox, his beekeeper's manual, a CD of a group he sang with in college, and an IRS manual that represented his career as a tax attorney.

At another friend's service there were costumes she'd made for a local little theater group, quilts she'd made, and photos of her with her children and grandchildren around her. At still another, the daughter of the deceased played the flute and friends read poetry, sang her favorite songs and danced as the dancer had performed for Mary Anne in the hospital the last week of her life.

At the other extreme, an elderly woman in our neighborhood died with no surviving children. Her nephew from out of state, the closest survivor, had the task of planning a funeral.

About all he knew about his aunt, whom he hadn't seen in years, was that she was Episcopalian. He arranged an elaborate religious ceremony, complete with incense, a choir and a processional and recessional. It was followed by a catered reception in the parish hall—very lightly attended, as the deceased had seldom attended church and few members even knew her. One friend lamented, "She would have been appalled at all the show."

Your Permanent Memorial

Do you want a permanent marker for your burial site? What kind? How large? Would you like a traditional rectangular shape, or something more elaborate, such as an angel?

 Put your wishes for a permanent memorial in writing.

I recently visited a Texas cemetery and stared amazed at some of the huge monuments—not to heroes of the Alamo, but to judges and businessman. On their tombstones were listed not only their names and dates of birth, as is traditional, but much more: degrees won, positions held, honors won, and in some cases, the names of all their offspring, with the degrees *they* had earned. It made for an interesting walking tour of the cemetery. If you—or your heirs—want to pay to have your resume set in stone, who am I to suggest that a scholarship in your name might be better?

After Tom's cremation, I arranged for his ashes to be scattered in a historic cemetery in the city where he'd grown up. For the scattering ceremony, I used the same wording that had been used for the church service, but there was no music, and those attending were mostly his childhood friends. A shrub was planted in his memory, with a plaque giving his name, dates of birth and death and a short epitaph: "Husband of Emilee, Father of Catherine and Friend of All." At the minister's suggestion, some of his ashes were also placed at his home, beside a rose bush he'd planted.

Whatever you decide on for your funeral and memorial, I hope the exercise has left you feeling proud of all you've accomplished in life thus far and all of the lives you've already touched. And don't forget: you've still got more time to add to both.

A funeral director in a retirement community said that new residents moved in, unpacked, opened a bank account, transferred their pre-paid funeral plans to their new town—and then proceeded to enjoy life for 20 more years.

Sample Funeral Plan

I want to be (buried/cremated)

If buried, I have purchased a cemetery plot at:

I want ___, ___, ___, ___, ___ and ___ as ushers.

I have arranged a pre-paid funeral with:
    Address & Phone #

Funds for my funeral service are in account _____ at _____

I want my memorial service to be held at _____

I want a viewing of my body ___Yes ___No

I want to be buried in my _____ (clothing). It is hanging in ____.

Flowers I want:

Music I want:

Special readings:

On my tombstone, I'd like:

Checklist for Chapter 13

☐ Check with the laws of your state to determine what options you have: burial, cremation, donation or other means of disposing of your body.

☐ Learn what facilities are near you for the method you've chosen.

☐ Write down what your choice is, and what facility you'd like to use.

☐ If you plan to have all or part of your body donated, make those arrangements now.

☐ If you'd like to be buried, choose a site and buy a burial plot, preferably in an established cemetery that has ongoing upkeep.

☐ If you'd like to be buried, designate what clothes you'd like to be buried in and put your chosen clothing in a place where it can be found, with a label indicating its purpose.

☐ If you'd like a traditional funeral and burial, go to funerals.org to learn about your options and what they're likely to cost.

☐ Write down your wishes regarding a viewing.

☐ Write down exactly what you want for your final ceremony.

☐ Put your wishes for your permanent memorial in writing.

☐ Place all of your instructions for your funeral in your file "In the Event of My Death."

Part II:
After
The
Loss

CHAPTER 14
"WHAT DO I DO NOW?"

In the instant when someone you love—especially your spouse—passes from life, your world changes forever. Death may have come suddenly, or it may have been a welcomed release after a long illness, but it will still be a shock, in the way that running blindly into a brick wall would be.

This person has been your companion, your lover, your confidant, the parent of your children. Now all that is gone. You are alone, with duties and responsibilities and a new unfamiliar role to play.

Ripples go out from you, affecting family, friends and business associates. Soon, the legal system, financial organizations and even the government will claim a large part of your daily life.

You may be stunned at first almost to paralysis, or you may throw yourself into a frenzy of activity. More likely you'll experience a combination of these. You may do and say strange things that are out of character for you. Others may say strange things to you. Forgive yourself and them. This is not a normal time.

During the first days of your bereavement, your role will be threefold: notify, arrange and accept. All of this will be easier if you have gone through the preparatory steps covered in the first part of our book. If you're beginning here, it will be more difficult, but this second part will help you get through the worst time of your life.

Notifying the Authorities

⚡ Immediately after a death, authorities must be notified.

If your beloved has died in a hospital, doctors will take care of notification and prepare a death certificate.

If death occurs outside a hospital, there are several possibilities of notification. Perhaps your spouse has had a long illness so that death is expected, but he/she dies at home. A call to the physician or the hospice person who has been caring for the patient is all that is necessary. My father-in-law died laughing while watching his favorite TV comedy. He'd recently been hospitalized for kidney failure and the family doctor lived nearby. The doctor certified that death had occurred and completed a death certificate.

You must notify the police in case of an accidental or "suspicious" death. This includes coming home to discover a loved one apparently dead, as well as horrible circumstances such as murder or suicide. Even less dramatic deaths may necessitate calling the police. A friend's mother was visiting her daughter, who came in from a brief trip to the supermarket to discover her mother collapsed by the door. Police asked probing questions, all but suggesting that the daughter might have wanted her mother dead. A coroner's examination determined that the cause of death was a massive stroke.

Despite the trauma of having police question you about the death of a loved one, establishing the cause of death will protect you in case someone later attempts to overturn a will.

In many unexpected deaths, an autopsy will be required by law. These include deaths due to murder, suicide or accident, or the sudden death of an otherwise healthy person.

Even though an autopsy is not required, there are circumstances when you may want to request one. For example, if the deceased has been ill of an undiagnosed ailment. Both you and the Centers for Disease Control may want to know the cause of death. Or he/she may have been a participant in a new drug or device experiment or there is the suspicion of hereditary illness that others should be aware of. Or you may wish to establish a cause of death for insurance purposes. For example, the deceased may have had double indemnity insurance or a cancer policy. Or the policy may have excluded suicide, and that possibility needs to be ruled out.

> If the deceased wanted to be an organ or body donor, this must be arranged immediately.

There is only a brief window during which the organs are viable. Hospital staff may ask you if you are willing to have the deceased's organs donated, even if there is no donor card signifying his/her intent. Whether there is a donor card or not, the nearest of kin must sign for the organs to be removed and the donation made.

Perhaps the deceased planned to donate his/her body to a medical school and made arrangements ahead of time for it. In this case, notify the institution immediately so that they may collect it as soon as possible after the autopsy, if any.

> Before the body is taken away, remove any jewelry.

And as ghoulish as it may seem, you can request the funeral home to remove gold teeth. The cremation society returned Tom's clothing and watch to me, but it's easy at such an emotional time to overlook jewelry. An ad runs regularly in our local newspaper offering a reward for the return of two rings worn by a woman who died in a nearby nursing facility.

Take the Next Steps

As soon as you've notified the legal and/or medical authorities, you'll probably want to notify your spiritual adviser, close family members and funeral director or cremation society.

If you've followed the first part of our book, you'll have a list of people to notify who will notify others. If either of you has a job, you must notify your employers and arrange for bereavement leave. You'll probably want to notify friends, family and business associates of the death immediately, with the message that you'll follow up later with details of the arrangements for a funeral or memorial service.

Or you may prefer to make the arrangements first before notifying others, to avoid unnecessary phone calls.

You will probably want to see your spiritual adviser (priest, rabbi, or other person who can help you cope). If you are planning a funeral or memorial service, you most certainly will.

Cremation vs. Burial

Do you want cremation or burial? If the deceased will be cremated within 24 hours, no embalming is required. However, if you plan on having a viewing of the body, then you must agree to embalming. Obviously, immediate cremation is a less expensive option than burial, since no coffin or vault is required, and no cemetery plot.

If you have not discussed this beforehand with your spouse and have no funeral or memorial service already planned, you'll need to make some quick decisions.

If you haven't chosen a funeral home, call several in the area and ask about services they offer and at what price.

There is nothing wrong with comparison shopping. If you can't bear to do this yourself, designate a trusted friend for this job, and let him or her know how much you are prepared to spend. In addition to the coffin and vault (which is required not to "protect" the body, but to keep the earth from sinking in as the coffin rots), you'll also be charged for opening and closing the grave, limos and hearse for transport, printed funeral cards and service sheet, and a viewing and service at the funeral home if you request this. You'll also need to decide if you want a funeral procession to and from the place of the service and to the site of the burial.

Such a funeral can cost $10,000 or more, vs. about $1,000 for cremation. If the burial is to be at some distant spot, the costs can skyrocket.

I recommend cremation for many reasons: there will be one fewer grave to take up space (and in some countries space is already at such a premium that the dead are buried atop one another, or are buried only temporarily), cremation is less expensive, it's less complicated and less emotional.

Don't be swayed into choosing something more elaborate than you can afford. You may be urged to spend lavishly, as in, "This shows how much you care." It doesn't. Your lifetime together showed how much you cared. Another suggestion you'll hear is, "He deserves the best." He/she cannot possibly benefit from an expensive coffin, however deserving he or she was.

 Whether you choose burial or cremation, at this point you must authorize the cremation society or funeral home to remove the body, and perform whatever services you request.

Checklist for Chapter 14

☐ Notify the authorities if the death occurred outside a hospital.

☐ Make arrangements for organ donation if the deceased wanted to be a donor.

☐ Notify the appropriate institution if the deceased wanted to donate his/her whole body.

☐ Request an autopsy if appropriate.

☐ Notify the appropriate funeral home or cremation society

☐ Authorize the removal of the body

☐ Remove any jewelry from the body

☐ Notify immediate family members

☐ Notify your spiritual adviser

CHAPTER 15
THE FIRST WEEK

Once you've gotten through the first terrible day following the death of your spouse, your next step is deciding what kind of funeral or memorial service you want, if any.

Planning the Funeral

For guidance in planning a funeral, see Chapter 13, "It's Your Funeral," or locate the wishes the deceased had written. If no plans have been made, you'll need to consider if you want a religious or secular service. Where will it be held? When? Who might attend? Will there be special music? If you are using a funeral home, observances must be coordinated with your minister or other religious leader and the site where the service will be held.

Funeral directors take care of practical matters, but if you are using a cremation society, you or your helpers will need to take care of much of this. For example, is there adequate parking at the site you have chosen for the service? Who will direct the parking? Will there be a procession through public streets or roads? In this case, the local traffic police will need to be notified. You may also need or wish to provide maps to the site.

As to the timing of the service, be led by your own wishes

and the necessary travel arrangements distant mourners must make, not the convenience of the funeral director or staff of your church. Your religion may require a very quick burial. Otherwise, nothing is lost by postponing a funeral or memorial service until it is the right time for you. Your beloved will not be any more dead next week than this week.

Tom had just had surgery when word came of his mother's death. He postponed her service until he was able to travel. Then his death occurred the Sunday before Thanksgiving. Our priest wanted to have the memorial service the following Sunday afternoon so that the organist would not have to return early from her beach house. My sister wisely pointed out that the Sunday after Thanksgiving was the busiest travel day of the year and given the short days, out-of-towners would be traveling not only in heavy traffic but in darkness.

We settled on Saturday, and the organist graciously drove several hours for the service, then returned to complete her holiday. Had this not worked out, we could have postponed the memorial service an additional week, since he was cremated and there was no burial.

With cremation you may have a memorial service soon after death and another later when the deceased's ashes are scattered or interred. There is no rush about either of these. Be guided by your own feelings. One friend has never had a memorial service for her husband, who died more than a decade ago, because he requested, "No service until you can get through it without crying." She has never reached that state, though she did have an informal service when his ashes were scattered.

 If you or the deceased had prepaid funeral arrangements, locate the policy to take with you to the funeral home.

 If you are having a burial instead of cremation,

you'll also need to locate the deed to the cemetery plot where the burial is to take place.

 Make an appointment with the funeral home to go over the specific arrangements, and at this time take along the clothing you wish the deceased to be viewed and buried in.

This should be some clothing the deceased had worn and felt comfortable in. It's unnecessary and wasteful to buy new clothing for a corpse. If the deceased is female, take along whatever makeup she wore, so that the funeral director can prepare her for viewing looking as natural as possible.

If the deceased wore a hairpiece and/or dentures, but was not wearing them at the time of death, take them to the funeral home as well. They will be no use to anyone else, but will make the deceased look more "natural."

Don't take eyeglasses. These can be used by a living person, and are of no use to the deceased. I have viewed corpses at funeral homes wearing glasses, and I wanted to snatch them away to donate to a charity for sight-impaired people.

Since there would be no body or coffin in the church, our minister suggested a display of items important in Tom's life. Catherine and I discussed it, wrote out what we would like said about Tom, and gathered his college lacrosse letter sweater, his beekeeping manual, his IRS tax manual, his violin, a small tool box and a CD of a musical performance he had sung in. We topped this off with one of his bowties and his favorite hat, and the minister took a photo of the display, which I put in our photo album.

On the same visit to the church, we chose some of Tom's and my favorite hymns, which the congregation would sing during the service.

⚡ After the funeral arrangements are made, notify friends and relatives and have an obituary published in the appropriate places.

The Obituary

⚡ If your spouse prepared an obituary, locate it, read it over to make sure the statements still apply, make a good copy and see that it gets to the proper newspapers.

The funeral home or cremation society will take care of dispersing the news, but you must furnish them the correct information.

If no obituary has been written, look back at Chapter 12, "Remembering You," for aid in writing it. You may need to consult friends and family members to gather facts about the deceased, such as earlier activities and affiliations, and the correct names of relatives who should be listed.

⚡ The obituary should be sent to newspapers in the deceased's hometown, if it's different from the residence at time of death, as well as towns or cities where he/she attended college or worked.

Notifying Others

You might have a list of people from Chapter 11, "Make a List and Check It Twice," who would want to know of the death but might not live in areas covered by the newspapers.

⚡ If you have their email addresses, compose a simple statement and send it to them all, or have a friend take care of this.

If there is little likelihood that they would plan to attend the funeral service or would need to know quickly, you might prepare a simple note to send sometime within the next month. It might even be part of your annual holiday newsletter if you send these to distant friends.

The first outsiders I notified of Tom's death were the administrators of the college where he was teaching an evening class. The college dean said she'd never had a faculty member die, but she didn't foresee any problems. Since he'd been paid for teaching the course, it would be my responsibility to pay whoever completed the final two sessions on his behalf. As we had planned a cruise that began two days before the exam, Tom had already arranged for a colleague to administer and grade the exam. I called him and he came to our house. Together, we went over Tom's notes for the class, the exam and the answer sheet. We agreed on his fee.

Planning for Your Guests

After planning the funeral or memorial service, you'll need to consider a luncheon or other gathering before the funeral service and possibly a reception for afterward. The luncheon is likely to be informal, perhaps made up of food brought by friends, supplemented by take-out food. Accept offers of food. You will be too busy and distraught to cook.

The reception by its very nature will be more formal. Who will cater it? Where will it be held? Most churches have rooms suitable for receptions, and many now have funeral reception committees who are on standby to provide flowers, food and beverages, set up tables, serve the refreshments and clean up afterward. This is a valuable service, especially in communities where people have retired away from their adult children and longtime friends. If you take advantage of this service, you should make a suitable donation afterward.

Many communities have local caterers who will provide a suitable array of food on short notice. Your helpers can arrange this if you don't feel up to the task, and can suggest foods that might be brought by those who ask, "What can I do to help?" (More on this in the next chapter.)

I knew that Tom's service would be at the downtown Portsmouth church where we were members and where we had sung in the choir and served on the vestry, but I had not considered what to do about a reception. A choir member called and said she'd be responsible for arranging the reception, and another said that instead of food, she wanted to provide flowers for the table. I gratefully accepted both.

Because church members and others were so gracious in arranging the reception for Tom's service, I now serve on the funeral reception committee at my present church. I can't repay those who served me, but I can "pay it forward," helping some other grieving spouse.

I consulted another friend and fellow church member, Sarah Kerr, a florist, about what flowers we would need. She said, "Leave it to me. I think just white orchids on the altar." Knowing her good taste, I accepted her choice.

You may also want or need to shop for clothing to wear to the service and reception, and you will probably need to arrange accommodations for out-of town family and friends who will come for the service.

 If you're hosting a reception or luncheon at your home, or housing out-of-town guests, arrange to have your house cleaned.

Don't try to do it yourself right now. (This might also be a

great suggestion for a friend or group who wants to do something to help but isn't sure what to do.)

Copies of the Death Certificate

 When you visit the funeral home or cremation society, buy as many copies of the death certificate as
you think you'll need.

I started with 10, and soon found that I needed 10 more.
Most businesses will only accept notarized certificates stamped
with the official seal, so you can't save money by making your
own copies. Notarized death certificates will cost $10 or more
each.

All this is emotionally traumatic and time-consuming. Remember that you don't have to do everything on this chapter's
checklist yourself; some of these items can be delegated.

In addition to these tasks, I had to cancel a cruise scheduled
for the following week. Parts of those days are still a blank, but
friends assured me I handled everything as I should have.

So can you.

Checklist for Chapter 15

☐ Meet with your spiritual adviser.

☐ Visit the cremation society or funeral home to discuss specific arrangements.

☐ Locate the deed to the cemetery plot and any paperwork for a prepaid funeral.

☐ Make arrangements for a memorial service.

☐ Decide on flowers and music.

☐ Write the deceased's obituary and arrange its publication.

☐ Arrange for out-of-town guests.

☐ Shop for necessary clothing and household goods such as paper napkins.

☐ Arrange for your house to be cleaned.

☐ Buy many copies of the death certificate.

CHAPTER 16
"WHAT CAN I DO TO HELP?"

When a death occurs, family and friends will come to comfort you, and many of them will say, "What can I do to help?" or "Let me know if there is anything I can do."

You'll probably want to say, "nothing," for there is nothing anyone can do to take away the sting of your grief. Your friends and family feel this helplessness, but they want to do something, and there are many practical things people can do to help you at this time.

Accept their help. It will be good for you and for the giver of help.

There are many ways people can help. Some of my suggestions were tasks that friends offered, others those that I requested when someone asked, "What can I do to help?"

Before the Funeral

 You'll need someone to answer the phone and door and record deliveries of flowers and food.

 You'll probably need housing for out-of-town mourners, and will want to arrange a luncheon, reception or some other social gathering.

If a funeral home is in charge of arrangements, your job will be easier, as they will see to visitation details, parking for the service, displays of flowers, etc. However, you might want some help in selecting a casket. Cremation societies don't handle these details, so you'll want to accept offers of help for these tasks.

> Record in your notebook (or the register furnished you by the funeral home or cremation society) who does what tasks for you, who sent which flowers, etc. It's easy to overlook something at time like this, and you'll want this list later when you write thank-you notes.

> Make a trip to the bank and get $100 or so in small bills. This is not to pay friends for helping you, but to pay for the things they will buy at your request, such as gasoline for your car, picking up your dry cleaning, paper and plastic serving utensils, etc.

> You may be too emotional to talk to callers on the phone, so assign someone to answer the telephone at your home and take messages. Keep a note pad by the phone for this purpose.

Food

The first item that most people offer is food. Especially in the South, friends show up with casseroles and desserts, and these will be useful for out of town guests. You will be too frazzled to cook, and visitors will be unaccustomed to your kitchen.

> The person who offers to help out with food should record in your notebook a description of the dish that was brought, the donor, and the container, as "chicken and rice casserole, in glass dish with lid, by

Marge Smith."

When Tom died, Rita Vaughan, one of my fellow church members, called to ask if this was a good time to visit, and when she visited, said, "I'd like to bring you four dozen ham biscuits." I accepted immediately. Ham biscuits are suitable for any meal, especially in the South, and they can be frozen for later use, a real plus when your counters fill up with perishable dishes. After Tom's service, his nephews from Ohio packed a "lunch" to sustain them on the long drive home from Virginia, and took the last of the ham biscuits. Rita's gift was thus doubly appreciated.

> Most offers won't be so specific, but if anyone suggests food and offers you a choice, request that the food be in disposable containers you won't have to keep track of and return.

And, like the ham biscuits, anything that can be frozen for later use is good. It can be quickly thawed if more guests show up than you had expected.

Transportation

> A very useful task someone can perform is to prepare a map and driving directions for getting to your home, to the site of the service and to the burial site.

Keep a copy by the phone to be read to out-of-towners who may not have GPS systems. Or, one of your helpers may email or fax directions. Have multiple copies available for those who will be going from your home or neighborhood to the church or funeral home.

Other tasks people may do for you include getting your car washed or arranging parking at the site of the funeral service if your funeral home does not provide this. The cremation society did not, and this was a specific task I could assign when someone offered help.

Without being asked, our next-door neighbors on one side cut the grass, and neighbors on the other side raked up fallen leaves while Catherine and I were shopping for black clothing.

The Day of the Funeral

The day of Tom's funeral service, a longtime friend, Rosa Leonard, and her husband Howard arrived at the house two hours before the luncheon. I was still in my robe and slippers. I thought I had everything taken care of, but I was wrong.

While Howard played with our grieving cocker spaniel and made a fire in the fireplace, Rosa put on an apron and set to work. "Show me where everything is," she said, "and then go take a shower and get dressed. I'll start cutting up things." She sliced cake, diced fruit and arranged platters on the buffet table. It was a valuable service. I had thought I had plenty of time to do everything, but I couldn't have managed without her.

> Another task you'll need to assign is for someone to stay at the house while you are at the funeral service.

The date and time of the service will have been publicized, so many people will know that your house is empty. Tom's niece's fiancé, Bob, had never met Tom, so he offered to stay behind instead of attending the service, an offer I gratefully accepted. Bob also wrapped and refrigerated leftovers, and loaded the dishwasher.

After the Funeral

Later, in weeks to come, a friend who offers help can cancel magazine subscriptions and notify the three credit bureaus of your spouse's death. Friends can also help by taking your deceased's clothing to charity thrift shops, or wrap and mail special items that have been promised to others. They may address thank-you notes, but you should do the actual writing, adding personal information.

If your spouse was employed, a helper can pack items from his/her workplace for you.

And after the service is over and the mourners have gone, special friends may call and invite you to lunch or a movie or play.

Accept.

Checklist for Chapter 16

Tasks you may assign:
- ☐ Answer phone and door
- ☐ Run errands
- ☐ Clean house
- ☐ Record food items and flowers, with descriptions
- ☐ Look up information on motels
- ☐ Prepare maps
- ☐ Arrange reception
- ☐ Stay at your house during the service
- ☐ Cancel subscriptions
- ☐ Write acknowledgements
- ☐ Notify credit bureaus

CHAPTER 17
TAKING CARE OF BUSINESS

The last thing you want to do soon after your beloved's death is take care of business. It seems so crass. Nevertheless, it has to be done, for your financial security and your legal protection.

> As soon as possible you'll need to consult with your financial adviser or your attorney to find out just where you stand financially.

If you've listed your joint assets as suggested in Chapter 3, "What Are You Worth?", make sure that information is accurate and up-to-date. If a trust was set up for you, notify the trustee(s) to activate it.

Social Security

The funeral director or cremation society will notify the Social Security Administration of the death, and Social Security will notify your bank to return any further checks if the deceased was receiving benefits. Failure to cooperate with the Social Security Administration could later result in your being charged with fraud if checks continue to arrive and be cashed. Our newspaper just this week had an article about a woman who did not report her husband's death a decade ago, but instead buried him in the back yard and continued accepting his Social Security checks.

If neither of you receives benefits but the deceased was employed, Social Security will also need to be notified of the death to prevent anyone else from using that Social Security number.

The cremation society notified Social Security of Tom's death, and Social Security in turn notified our bank where his checks had been deposited. His next check, due only a few days after his death, was withheld, and within a week the local Social Security office called me for an appointment to determine if I was due any "benefits" from Tom's death.

Prepare for Legal and Financial Matters

Your bank should be alert to prevent any fraudulent checks or automatic withdrawals made in the name of the deceased. You may want to set up a new account, to be called "The Estate of …."

 Within the next few days, cancel any doctor's or other appointments and notify medical personnel of the death.

 You may need to also see your legal adviser at this time.

He or she may have the original of the deceased's will. It is traditional to read the will to the gathered heirs after a service, especially if they have traveled a great distance. If you own everything jointly and are thus the only heir, there is no reason to read the will to anyone.

For all the legal and financial matters you'll be dealing with in the coming weeks, you'll need copies of the Death Certificate. If you did not order enough copies through the funeral home or cremation society, you may later reorder from the court in the jurisdiction where the death occurred. In my case, Tom died in Newport News, we lived in Portsmouth, and the cremation society was in Virginia Beach.

You need not probate the will at this time. Not yet.

Know What Changes as a Result of Death

Mortgage

 Determine the status of your mortgage and any other joint loans.

Do they fall due upon the death of your spouse? If so, you'll have to refinance, which is tedious enough to do at any time, but especially difficult for you as a newly widowed person. Your credit rating may have been tied to the earnings of your spouse and without him/her, your own credit rating may not qualify you for a low-rate mortgage.

You may have mortgage insurance—essentially a life insurance policy that pays off your mortgage upon the death of the holder. Many financial advisers consider this an expensive and wasteful kind of insurance, but homeowners who have needed it might disagree. There's no financial security like having a paid-for home.

Partnerships

Was your spouse involved in a business partnership? Does it dissolve upon his or her death? Do you need to buy out the other partner or sell to him/her? You'll need to see a lawyer about this. The proceeds from a business may have made up a good part of your income, which will now cease.

Insurance

Is there insurance? If you have followed our suggestions in Chapter 11, you have a list of insurance policies, their amounts, and a phone number of the party to contact for payment. If you are newly widowed and reading this for the first time, search through files and desk drawers and in the safe deposit box for possible policies.

 List each policy in your notebook, note the date you called, the person you spoke to, and what documentation (usually a death certificate), you must provide in order to collect on the claim.

 Ask if you can fax a copy of the death certificate.

The Veterans Administration, for one, allowed this on Tom's insurance. Usually, the insurance company will send you a form to be filled out and returned along with a notarized or certified copy of the death certificate.

 If you don't hear within two weeks, make a follow-up call. This is money you are entitled to. If the deceased died in an accident, you may have to submit a copy of the police and/or emergency response report.

Pensions and Retirement

Do you have enough money to live on? If not, you may need to move to smaller quarters. Did your spouse receive a pension? Does that end with his/her death, or will you continue to receive money from it? How much? (In some cases, the pension will continue unless/until you remarry.) You'll need to contact the source of the pension to find out.

If the deceased had a pension, contact the pension

plan to learn its details.

Before I retired, I'd signed what the school personnel director called "the sweetheart deal," which she said most employees wanted. In return for my taking a smaller amount of pension each month after I retired, Tom would receive half my monthly pension for the remainder of his life if I died first. He was also the beneficiary of my required life insurance policy.

Soon after Tom died, I called the Virginia Retirement System to report the death. I was able to revert to what I would have received. I got no refund for the time I'd taken less, of course. That's the way the system operates. Insurance is all about playing the odds, or covering both possibilities.

I was able to get a refund on Tom's health insurance. About three months after his death I noticed that automatic payment of premiums for both of us were still being deducted from the bank account. I called the insurance company, who refunded the payments retroactively back to the day of his death, since he would no longer be requiring medical care.

Planning for Your New Financial Situation

Budgeting

After you have located possible sources of income, it's budget time.

 Make a list of all your regular expenses, which may involve searching the files or going through bank statements, especially if your spouse was the family bookkeeper and money manager.

 Divide a piece of paper down the center; label the left side "Income" and the right side "Expenses."

On the left side, list your expected income, including what you earn, your monthly Social Security payment, monthly pension and/or annuity and one-twelfth of the annual amount you are required to withdraw from your IRA if you are over 70 years old.

On the right side, list the regular expenses incurred for the household: utilities, dues, charitable contributions usually made or pledged, any insurance premiums (these may come quarterly, in which case you'll need to divide the payment amount into thirds to arrive at the amount you must allow for each month), car expenses, groceries and other regularly purchased items.

If you have trouble arriving at these figures, go back through bank statements and charge card statements to determine how money has been spent in previous months. Some of these items will be less for you alone. You'll consume less food, and if you have two cars, you can certainly dispense with one.

 If your costs are more than your income, see what expenses you can cut.

One that you can't cut is the cost of the funeral. You chose and committed to it, and it must be paid now, along with any medical costs of the deceased's last illness. You may also have chosen a marker or tombstone for the grave and will need to arrange to pay for it and have it put in place. Most wills specify that these debts must be paid before any disbursements can be made from the estate.

Credit

 As soon as you can arrange to do so, notify the three credit-rating agencies, Experion, Equifax and TransUnion that your spouse has died.

 Check his/her credit rating. There should be no

further changes in the rating, as the deceased can incur no further debts, and after the notification, neither can identity thieves use his/her information.

Checklist for Chapter 17

☐ Consult with your attorney and/or financial adviser to determine your financial standing.

☐ Activate any trusts.

☐ Check the terms of your mortgage.

☐ Locate insurance policies and request claim forms.

☐ Notify medical personnel and health insurance companies of the death.

☐ Check the terms of the deceased's pension.

☐ Make a budget to determine your financial options.

☐ Notify the three credit-rating bureaus of the death.

CHAPTER 18
IT'S THE LAW

Erma Bombeck once wrote, "Even death is no excuse for not filing a tax return." Not only is it not an excuse, death is actually a *cause* of your having to file numerous pieces of legal paper. Some are required by the laws of your state. Others will benefit you, bringing in much-needed funds.

Wills

The first document you must deal with is the will.

 As soon as possible after a death, determine if the deceased left a will.

Many people don't make a will, and in some states if you are the surviving spouse, you will have an automatic right to a certain portion of the estate without a will. However, if yours was a second or later marriage, if there are adult children or if you have signed a prenuptial agreement, you could find that you are one of several heirs. In most states, a surviving spouse cannot be totally disinherited, but you could be left with very little.

 If the will is in the care of an attorney, contact him or her and arrange to read the will, accompanied by a trustworthy person.

If you are not the named executor, contact the person who is. Get the original will and make copies for all heirs who are named. This does not have to be the dramatic setup depicted in books and movies, when someone gasps as he or she is 'cut out' of a big legacy, or surprisingly named the inheritor of a fortune.

Are you are named as executor, or is someone else? Is that person willing to carry out the terms of the will? If not, is the alternate willing to do so? If neither is, then the court may appoint an administrator. Both executors and administrators are entitled to a fee, depending on the size of the estate. This is usually set by law, but it may be negotiated for a different amount. If you are not the executor, don't begrudge the named executor a fee. Settling an estate, especially if there are numerous heirs and bequests, can be a time-consuming business.

If you are the executor and the estate is simple, you may be able to handle it yourself without an attorney. Call up the clerk of court in your city, town or county to find out how long a time after a death you have to register the will. In Virginia, it was 30 days.

Tom and I owned everything in common ("joint owners with survivorship" is the legal term for this) except for the two cars, which were in his name alone. Since both our cars were used, their value was minimal, so there was no estate tax. I had to pay only the registration fee to the city. The procedure of registering the will took about an hour, and I purchased extra copies of the registration certificate. If Tom had left personal property with a high value, I would have had to pay an estate tax, and may have had to probate the will.

Probate

Not all wills need to be probated. Probate means "to

prove"—in this case, to the satisfaction of the court that you have accounted for the deceased's property and are dispensing it according to his/her wishes.

If you are the executor and there are other heirs, the procedure will be more complicated.

 First, you will need to advertise for any creditors.

If the deceased left unpaid bills, this is the opportunity for the creditors to come forth and show proof of money owed. If you don't locate creditors but settle the estate anyway and creditors later come forth, you may be held personally responsible for paying the bills owed by the deceased.

A sample of a legal notice for creditors is at right.

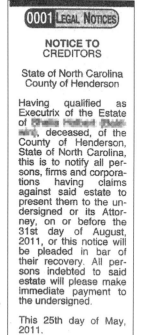

 Second, as executor, you will need to take an inventory of the estate and estimate the value of each item as of the date of death.

This inventory must be presented to the clerk of court. If you and the deceased have followed the instructions in the earlier part of this book, your job is fairly simple. If not, see Chapter 3, "What Are You Worth?"

It's helpful to keep all your records for the estate in a loose-leaf binder with pockets to hold receipts, bills and other loose papers.

0001 LEGAL NOTICES

NOTICE TO CREDITORS

State of North Carolina
County of Henderson

Having qualified as Executrix of the Estate of ███ ███ ███ ███, deceased, of the County of Henderson, State of North Carolina, this is to notify all persons, firms and corporations having claims against said estate to present them to the undersigned or its Attorney, on or before the 31st day of August, 2011, or this notice will be pleaded in bar of their recovery. All persons indebted to said estate will please make immediate payment to the undersigned.

This 25th day of May, 2011.

 You'll need to secure the assets immediately. Do not let anyone take away any of the deceased's property, claiming, "He always said this would be mine when he died."

You as executor are accountable for the property, and failure to divide assets equitably is responsible for many family feuds that split siblings or even child from parent.

 Armed with a copy of the will naming you as executor and a copy of the death certificate, freeze any bank accounts and brokerage accounts owned solely by the deceased.

Search for bank statements or other proof of accounts, and if necessary, call local banks where you suspect the deceased may have had accounts. Open and inventory safe deposit boxes. Locate property deeds, if necessary by calling the clerk of court or the tax commissioner's office. The person to whom the tax bill is sent is generally the owner. Taxing authorities are willing to help you settle an estate, so taxes can be assessed on the new owner rather than from an estate.

 In your inventory, list all the real estate, giving its recent appraised value.

This can be determined by the latest tax bill or by having a professional appraisal done. Next, list the amount in bank accounts; any loans owed to the deceased; and stocks, bonds and mutual funds the deceased owned. For stocks and bonds, list the closing price on the day of death. To get an accurate value for these, locate a copy of the *Wall Street Journal* for the date of death and check the prices.

 Next, search the deceased's jewelry box and chests to find valuable personal items, such as cufflinks or rings, especially if those are mentioned in the will as bequeathed to a specific person.

When Tom's aunt died, her will specified that two described

rings were to go to a great niece, but Tom could never find the rings. The aunt had known for some time that the rings were missing, and had accused certain family members of taking them, but had not changed her will to omit them as a bequest. Had the aunt lost them or sold them? Had they been carelessly thrown out in the trash? We never knew. If you no longer have an item, take it out of your will.

In the case of art, musical instruments and jewelry, you as executor may have to pay an appraiser to get an accurate valuation. Do so, to avoid misunderstanding or quarrels later. The cost of the appraisal, along with funeral expenses and the executor's fee, will be deducted from the estate before bequests are made.

For complicated estates, settling probate may take a year or more.

Settling and Closing Accounts

 Write a letter—and always keep a copy—to brokerage firms canceling the deceased's account.

If you own the account jointly, notify the brokerage firm of the death, but don't close the account. A further caveat: find out whose Social Security number was listed first on the account, and if it is that of the deceased, request in writing that it be transferred to you as joint owner.

I found this out the hard way when I attempted to sell some stock a few months after Tom's death and was told legally I couldn't, though I had been the deciding one on stock purchases and sales for years, and even served on the church vestry with the broker. Tom's Social Security number was the one used to identify the account for tax purposes, not mine, since he was considered the head of household. By the time the account had been transferred solely to my name and Social Security number, the stock had dropped substantially in price. Ignorance of the law is not bliss, and it certainly is not profitable.

Don't close joint bank accounts, but do notify all banks and credit unions with which you did business of the death, even though Social Security will have notified the bank to which benefit checks were sent.

 If at all possible, go in person and make sure the bank has samples of your signature and that of the deceased.

This will prevent an unauthorized person from representing himself as the deceased and withdrawing money. At the same time, keeping the account open will allow you to deposit any checks made out to the deceased that may arrive after the death. For these checks, you must sign the name of the deceased, by you, or have a stamp made with the name of the deceased and the words "For Deposit Only." One check that will arrive is the terribly named "death benefit," currently $255, from Social Security.

 It's a good idea at this time to add the name of some other trustworthy person to the account, in case of your own death or disability.

This may be a child, a sibling, or someone else you designate. That person must accompany you to the bank and complete a signature card. If you don't want him/her writing checks in the meantime, specify that the check-writing power begins "in the event of my death."

You must have an appointment with Social Security if you or the deceased received benefits or if you have minor children who will now receive benefits. You will need to bring with you a copy of your marriage license, the death certificate, and both your Social Security numbers as well as any other papers requested. This interview will determine if you will receive benefits based on the decedent's work history or your own.

Other Legal Repercussions of Death

Other laws will apply here as well. In spite of jokes to the contrary, you will need to take the decedent's name off the voter rolls.

 Call up the local registrar and ask to have the deceased's name removed.

In some states this is automatic, when the death is reported to the Bureau of Vital Statistics, but in other states you may need to write a letter to the registrar, include a copy of the death certificate and turn in the decedent's voter registration card.

Automobiles

Transferring the titles of cars the deceased owned can be tricky.

I donated the car Tom had driven most of the time to the Salvation Army, and that was easy. I removed the license plates and left the vehicle in the driveway with the title on the front seat. I was purposely away from home when the charity came for the car, so that I would not see it towed away. When I returned, the driveway was empty, and a few days later I received a copy of the canceled title and a statement of its value.

Transferring title of the car I usually drove from him to me took two visits to the Department of Motor Vehicles, armed with the title, a copy of the death certificate and a reading of the mileage. This transfer was treated as a "sale." At that time I surrendered the license plates to his car that I had donated, vanity plates that bore his initials and canceled his driver's license.

He was ceasing to exist legally.

Rental Property

We had purchased rental property in Texas when our daughter attended the University there, and I decided to sell it. Tom had always done the bookkeeping for the property, made sure repairs were done, and kept in touch with the manager. I didn't want to do any of those things.

Luckily, I had a call from a realtor who had interested buyers, and I listed with him. The manager, also a realtor, protested that he should have had the listing. He instructed the tenants not to allow any potential buyers or renters to view the condos. I had to send certified letters to him and to the tenants stating that their leases required them to make the property available for inspection and showing. In the case of the manager, I followed it up with a letter threatening to report him to the Texas Board of Realtors unless he cooperated.

The stress didn't end when the property soon sold. I went to Texas for the closings—armed with a couple of copies of the death certificate—a checkbook, copies of the deeds and rental leases. Even this was not enough.

Apparently there had been problems of people claiming to be widowed so they could sell property without their spouse's consent. I was given papers to take back to Virginia to have signed and notarized by friends and neighbors who could attest that we had had a "valid marriage." I protested that anyone who could attest to what went on in another's marriage would be committing perjury. Eventually the real estate board allowed me to sign a statement of my own, attesting that I had been married to Tom for 37 years. I raised my hand and swore that I was telling the truth, and handed over a copy of the death certificate to attach to the statement.

Taxes

Then came the tax return. Tom had been a tax attorney, had worked for a tax prep firm and had filed our returns electronically. I could not find a paper copy of the previous year's return, and called the IRS. I talked to an actual person and gave her our Social Security numbers. A few days later a copy of our previous return arrived. Some months later I found the tax return and backup materials in a box in our cluttered garage. This extra work could have been avoided if we'd had a specific place to put such papers.

On a sad day in March I sat in the tax preparer's office and signed a return that represented the income and deductions of "Thomas B. Cantieri (Deceased) and Emilee H. Cantieri."

This was Tom's last legal document.

Checklist for Chapter 18

☐ As soon as possible after a death, determine if the deceased left a will.

☐ If the will is in the care of an attorney, contact him or her and arrange to read the will, accompanied by a trustworthy person.

If you are the executor:

☐ Advertise for any creditors.

☐ Take an inventory of the estate and estimate the value of each item as of the date of death.

☐ Keep all your records for the estate in a loose-leaf binder with pockets to hold receipts, bills and other loose papers.

☐ Secure the deceased's assets as soon as possible; don't let anyone take anything because "she always told me I could have it when she died."

☐ Freeze any bank accounts and brokerage accounts owned solely by the deceased. (You'll need a copy of the will and the death certificate.)

☐ Write a letter—and always keep a copy—to brokerage firms canceling the deceased's account.

☐ If at all possible, go in person and make sure the bank has samples of your signature and that of the deceased.

☐ Call up the local registrar and ask to have the deceased's name removed.

CHAPTER 19
TAKING CARE OF YOURSELF

There is no such thing as "normal" behavior when your life's partner has died. All grief is universal, but your grief is also your own and individual. Don't be swayed by too much advice from well-meaning friends as to what you "ought" to do. You may appear to others to be totally in control while you are breaking apart inside, or you may be unable to control your tears or to carry on your usual duties.

You may do and say some things that in retrospect will appear strange, even bizarre. At Tom's memorial service, I saw his close friend alone at the rear of the church, and went back to ask if he'd like to sit with the family. I didn't mean beside me, but he squeezed into the front pew before I could sit back down, and other mourners wondered who he was and what I was doing. I may have done other bizarre things and not remembered them.

Nothing you do or say can change the awful thing that has altered your life, but there are some things you can do that will help you get through the days and weeks ahead.

Getting Through the Day and Night

You may need a sedative to sleep at first, but try to wean yourself off medication as soon as possible. If you are accustomed to having an evening cocktail or wine with dinner, continue your pattern, but don't look on alcohol as a way to assuage your grief.

I once attended the funeral of a colleague whose widow appeared serene throughout the service. She thanked us all for attending and smiled as she shook our hands. I remarked on this to another colleague who said, "She's smashed, and has been ever since he died." She eventually got off the booze, but the grief was still there to be dealt with. Alcohol had only postponed it.

Some grieving survivors want to withdraw from the world and nurse their grief in private, much as a wounded animal will seek its cave. Others are just the opposite, trying to keep grief at bay through activity. I was this kind.

Remember to Eat and Drink

I decided that I would get up at my usual time each morning, shower, get dressed and have a nourishing breakfast. Then no matter what the day brought, I would at least be clean, fed and alert. It was good for me to be prepared, as I had to answer the door numerous times and take care of many business details.

During this stage you may cry a great deal and forget to eat and drink, or lose your appetite altogether, thus becoming weak and dehydrated. Make a point of drinking enough water every day and going easy on the sweets and fatty foods. Grief delivers a traumatic blow to your whole system, not just your emotions. You're especially vulnerable to illness at this time, so take care of yourself.

Exercise

You may feel like pulling up the covers and never getting out of bed, but you need to make yourself take exercise. Barbara felt that one way to take care of herself was to follow her usual routine but to add strenuous exercise. When she was exercising, she said, she couldn't cry or think. She began by walking up the steep hill near her home. I was outside working in my garden one evening when she came past, her forehead glistening with perspiration. "I've done it," she said proudly. "I made it all the way up. At first I could only get part way up before I gave out. I'm back in shape again."

Physical exercise is good for several reasons, releasing endorphins that give an overall feeling of well-being. It also makes us feel that if we can push our bodies to perform, we are in control of other things as well.

If you don't want to walk by yourself, call up a friend who has offered to help you, and go for a brisk walk together. It may remind you of walks you've taken with your spouse, but you'll have to deal with those memories from now on.

Grief, Your New Companion

It's okay to talk about your deceased partner, but don't dwell morbidly on the death itself. My friend Pete confided that for months he couldn't talk about his late wife without crying, and he didn't think it was manly to cry so much. Eventually, when nearly a year had passed, he could talk about her and the good marriage they'd had, but by then his friends had moved on and no one wanted to talk about her. So cry, and talk, if it will help you. Real friends will help you through this time.

My method of handling grief was activity. I tried to finish up projects Tom had begun, and go on with volunteer work he had signed up for as well as my own usual activities. I arranged to have the heavy timbers moved into place for the garden beds Tom had laid out, and cleared up the remaining limbs from a late hurricane.

He always rang the bell for the Salvation Army on the first Saturday in December, and I went to ring the bell in his place. My writing group was scheduled to have the annual Christmas party at our house, and the president considerately offered to have it elsewhere. I went ahead with the party, but found myself in tears remembering how much Tom had enjoyed parties, and what a helpful, genial host he'd been.

I also had a book signing scheduled for two weeks after his death, and I went ahead with that as well. It was a disaster, though not because of my grief. The publisher had sent the wrong books but no one at the store had opened the cartons to check. The store had only three copies of my book in stock, so I wasted an afternoon and the store lost sales. I thought, 'Just wait until I tell Tom about this,' and then realized I never again could share anything with him.

You may think you see your deceased partner in a crowd, only to have the person turn and be someone else. You may hear his/her voice. You're not going crazy. Part of this is your own wish to have your beloved back, and part of it is that there are characteristics in many others that remind us of the one we loved. You may turn over in bed and fling out your arm to touch your partner, only to encounter emptiness, and realization.

You may dream about the deceased. I had two very Freudian dreams of Tom. In one he was slumped in a wheel chair while I tried to revive him and kiss him. In the other, he was late picking me up after a meeting and I started walking home, only to get hopelessly lost without him.

I thought I was adjusting admirably, and others told me so,

but one day in April, five months after his death, I started crying and couldn't stop. It was a lovely warm morning, the kind of day on which we'd have been setting out plants in the garden or taking a long walk. I called Ron, our minister, and asked him to come and talk with me. When he came, we walked in the garden and he said, "I was beginning to worry that you hadn't had this complete breakdown into tears. The longer you put off the crying, the longer it takes to stop. You should cry."

"But so many people are worse off," I said. "What about someone whose husband is murdered, or who had to take care of him through a terrible illness?"

"Don't compare yourself to anyone else," he said. "Your grief is just as painful to you no matter how Tom died. You have lost someone very precious to you. Your heart is broken, and crying will help it heal."

The Grief of Others

In your own grief, consider your children or grandchildren and pets. They don't understand death, but they miss the deceased and need comfort and reassurance from you.

We had adopted a cocker spaniel from the animal shelter, who had been "Tom's dog." Stokeley, as we named him, had been neglected by his original owners, tied daily in a driveway and banished to the garage at night, then finally left at the shelter. Tom had gone to pick him up, and then had taken him to the vet for his numerous ills, so Stokeley had bonded with Tom and followed him around. When we went walking, Tom usually handled Stokeley's leash, and taught him to play ball. I on the other hand gave him baths, poked pills down him and put drops in his eyes twice a day. No wonder he preferred Tom.

After Tom died, Stokeley wandered around looking for him

at all the places he'd shared with Tom: the garden, the car, the recliner, the storage shed-- and showed his grief by defecating on the rug by Tom's desk and again on the rug beside Tom's side of the bed. Stokeley was otherwise house trained and never had another "accident" before or after.

There is of course no way to explain death to an animal, but as a part of your own healing, you may want to share happy memories of the deceased with children. Avoid saying, 'Grandpa has gone to sleep and won't wake up.' This may cause children to fear going to sleep. Instead, say something like, 'Grandma has died and we'll never see her again, but we will think about her and how much she loved us.'

If you have older or adult children, they will be grieving as you are, and part of taking care of yourself will include letting them take care of you. Share good memories with them, and say how much you miss your beloved.

Self-Care

Taking care of yourself includes your mental health as well as your physical well-being. If you feel unable to cope, try to locate a grief counseling group. I did not attend any sessions, but my sister did when her husband died, and so have many others. Their experiences were positive, as they shared their feelings with others who had also been bereaved recently.

You are more prone to heart attacks and accidents at this time, so you should take extra precautions to stay safe. A startling number of people die within a year of their spouse's death.

David almost did. He didn't have to clean out the gutters. He could have asked a neighbor or his son for help, but he decided to do it himself. Part-way through the task, he fell off the ladder, rolled down the steep lawn and over a retaining wall, landing close beside the highway, battered and unconscious.

He regained consciousness in a hospital, with broken back, cracked ribs and a broken lower leg. His pastor had been driving past, saw him and called an ambulance. David was bitter that he had survived while his wife was dead. "My pastor said it was God's will that he came along when he did," David told me. "I told him that he and God should have let me die." David believed his fall was no accident, but his subconscious wish to die. He was put on suicide watch. Gradually his body healed and friends convinced him it was not his time to die.

The behavior and remarks of others may bother you more than usual. Many people just don't know what to say to the recently widowed, and you'll need to forgive them for their insensitive remarks. At the service where we scattered Tom's ashes, I asked if anyone would like to speak about Tom's life. One of his high school classmates recounted a long anecdote about her having remedial classes with the football team.

While Tom had been on the football team, I knew he had never taken any remedial classes. He'd been a top scholar and a member of the Honor Society. As Catherine later said, "I thought, 'This isn't a high school reunion. It's my Dad's funeral.'" An embarrassing incident also occurred at the service when we each took a handful of ashes to scatter. A breeze stirred suddenly, blowing some of Tom's ashes all over one of his classmates.

Take care of yourself, whatever it takes. You can recover your serenity, even your sense of humor. It may not seem so to you for a long time, but you will be able to laugh and enjoy life again. I doubted this, and said so to a friend who wrote, "Yes, you can laugh without guilt. I think it would make Tom glad to know that you were not continuously sad. Be well."

Make an effort to get out into the world. In the classic *Great Expectations*, Charles Dickens depicted the grotesque Miss

Havisham, who had locked herself away from the world, bitter and grieving her lost love, unable to move on. The news media regularly feature recluses who are found dead alone. We don't want to be either of those extreme cases. After an initial period, friends and relatives will go their way, living their own lives, and expecting you to look after yourself. And you can.

You are no longer part of a couple, but you are still a worthwhile person, and there are many people who need you and many things you would find worthwhile and interesting. Take a class in something new, or pick up a hobby you abandoned when your life was too busy. Volunteer at an animal shelter or a hospital, or teach someone to read. You will open up someone else's world as well as your own.

Checklist for Chapter 19

☐ Make yourself continue a "normal" routine of eating and sleeping.

☐ Take exercise, especially going for a walk where you'll see others.

☐ Take a sedative if necessary to fall asleep the first week, but wean yourself from using medications.

☐ Cry if you need to, and talk about your beloved.

☐ Remember that other family members and pets are grieving too, and need you.

☐ Make new friends and develop new interests.

CHAPTER 20
GRIEF IS NORMAL—AND STRANGE

Marriage Moon

Half a moon
shines above,

the other half
is shadowed

like our marriage.
Half has died

and my half
is still alive.

But the moon is solid, round.

Our marriage
is not broken

by death or night.
We circle earth

half in darkness,
half in light.

By Jeannette Carlberg Kaulfers, on observing a bright half-moon on Nov. 11, 2010, after the death of her husband, Tim.

When someone you love dies, there's no way you can go on as you were before. The center of your life has shifted and everything about you is affected: your health, your relationships with others, your emotions, your ability to make decisions or even to carry out simple, familiar tasks.

Friends may tell you to "snap out of it," or urge you to cry, or they—and you—may wonder why you are not crying more. You may think you are going crazy. As Bill said after his wife's death, "I felt like I was jumping out of my skin." There is no such thing as right or wrong reactions to death, and no "average." Every person grieves in his or her own way. For some, grief is a series of highs and lows, for others it is a dull ache that goes on for years. In some cultures, the bereaved wail, tear their hair and throw themselves on the ground. And some near-deranged ones have to be restrained from throwing themselves into the open grave.

The manner of the death may affect your grief. Your response may include horror at a violent death, guilt that you may have done something that caused the death or failed to do something that might have prevented it ("If only I had...") , relief that your loved one is free from pain, guilt at feeling relief or a numb emptiness.

Death After a Long Illness

Watching someone you love deteriorate, go through extensive treatments, improve and then die brings a different kind of grief from a sudden, unexpected death. During the long time from diagnosis until death, both the dying one and the spouse are riding an emotional rollercoaster. Maybe the diagnosis was wrong. When there is remission of disease, there is hope, and expectations rise, only to tumble at the next crisis. Gradually the realization sinks in that this person is going to die. Caregivers may be worn out physically, but still unwilling to let go. Maybe there will be a miracle. Maybe the next drug will work.

Bill's wife had a rare form of cancer, which could only be treated by a bone marrow transplant. Following the transplant she had chemo, then a second bone marrow transplant. During that year, she was in the hospital for six months, at home in good health for two months, and for the remaining four had outpatient tests and treatments.

It was a year of optimism, as the doctors always seemed to have another possible treatment to try, and as he said, "It was one of the closest times of our marriage." Then uncontrollable pneumonia set it, and the family converged from around the world, sharing pictures and memories for the last time.

The slow dying does give the spouse and family the opportunity to resolve issues, forgive each other, make peace with those they may be estranged from, and finally to express love and say goodbye.

Sudden Death

Not so with the sudden death. Tom had endured several debilitating conditions. Because of an inherited mitral valve weakness, he'd had a heart attack, followed by having a steel valve implanted in his heart. I was away on a trip to South America at the time, and learned of his heart attack and surgery in a phone call home from Ushaia, Argentina. If he'd died while I was away, my grief would have been worse, compounded by guilt.

As it was, I nursed him and watched him return from a frail, flabby heart patient to robust health. Nearly five years passed during which we went about our usual activities. Tom had narcolepsy as well, and when he failed to take his Ritalin on time, he could fall asleep suddenly. Whenever he was late coming home from work and hadn't called, I envisioned him having a fatal accident on the Virginia Beach Expressway.

He did die at the wheel of a vehicle, but it was barely moving, and narcolepsy was not the cause. His steel valve stopped ticking. He had complained of feeling cold in the weeks before his death, and had slept more than usual. After his death I wondered if I should have done something, if I should have been more observant, insisted that he see his cardiologist, even though he had been given the go-ahead two months before to do whatever he felt like.

There was no warning the day of his death that I was cooking his last breakfast, reading him a paragraph from the newspaper for the last time. He laughed and told jokes at breakfast, and chatted with a neighbor before he drove off in the rental van. We took slightly different routes, he waved jauntily, and he got to Catherine's apartment first. Then, a few hours later, he slumped over the wheel, made a strangled noise, and managed somehow to jerk the van's transmission into Park before he collapsed.

Later I took a CPR course and learned that the victim should lie flat with the head tipped back to clear air passages, and chest compressions should be started. I didn't know to do those things, and tortured myself with, "If only I'd known what to do, I might have saved his life." Tom's cardiologist assured me that nothing I did would have made any difference.

Our daughter Catherine felt guilty for allowing him to help her move, but the cardiologist told her it was Tom's choice. He'd been given a clean bill of health, told to do whatever he felt like doing. The doctor reminded us that Tom had had the presence of mind to drive himself to the emergency room when he had a heart attack, and if he'd had any inkling he was in danger of dying on that November afternoon, he'd have said so. Still, guilt dies hard when it's mixed with grief.

A friend wrote: "I felt guilt about the parts of our relationship we never worked through. It was a good relationship, but it had some glitches. It's taken me a while, but I've concluded that we were each imperfect, but pretty okay too. She was cheated out of years of life, but her glass was three-quarters full."

Suicide

The hardest of all to bear is the surviving spouse of a suicide. You will be bombarded with self-doubt and unanswered questions: Why didn't I sense that he/she was planning suicide? What could I have done to prevent it? Didn't he/she love me enough to want to go on living? Why didn't he/she seek help?

Being the one to find the beloved's body adds another layer of horror that may never be forgotten and will take years to recover from.

The survivors of suicides should definitely seek counseling. Their grief is of a different magnitude than mine was, for Tom loved life and continued to be active until his last moments, despite lifelong multiple health problems. I can feel sympathy for the surviving spouses or children of suicides, but I can't "put myself in their shoes."

Processing the Loss

My minister counseled me several times. "Tom died the way he would have wanted to," he said, and I felt he was right. Tom had seen his mother and mine linger for years after strokes, needing caregivers and slowly losing the characteristics that had made them the women we knew and loved. He dreaded having a stroke and being a burden. "If Tom could have been resuscitated, he would probably have spent the rest of his life in the hospital or a nursing home, and he'd have hated that," the minister consoled me. "And it would have killed you to see him like that." Intellectually, I knew it was true, but I wasn't ready to lose him. He'd only recently retired, and we had such plans for the next decade or two together.

This is a frequent feeling among survivors. Paul Jones wrote that he and Alexis had planned a cruise on the Amazon, the most adventuresome of many trips they'd enjoyed together. They'd assumed and planned that since he was older he would die first, and her sudden death hit him as "my world turned upside down."

People told me I was "strong," "composed." I wasn't. I was in a daze, almost like a robot. A few weeks after Tom's funeral I attended the funeral at our church of a friend, and hearing the same words that had been spoken for Tom, I broke down and sat with tears streaming down my face throughout the service. Bereaved people are urged to go on with ordinary activities, but attending a funeral so soon after Tom's was not a good idea.

A longtime friend whose wife had died a few months before Tom, sent me a tiny book given out in his grief counseling sessions, "Grief…reminders for healing," by Gale Massey, M.S. (Available from the author at P.O. Box 8945, Atlanta, GA 31106) One quotation in particular still brings tears: "You will forget they are gone and then remember again, and your heart will break one more time." This describes so well how difficult it is to believe, to accept that you will never see or hear or touch him/her again. And yet you must accept. You are still alive, and as Massey says, "that is how it should be."

The Effects of Grief

But you are not yourself. Nearly everyone I talked with had insomnia in the weeks following the death of a spouse. I kept awakening at 4 a.m., unable to sleep more than a few hours each night.

For Bill, a research scientist, the death took away his ability to concentrate. He'd long enjoyed reading before bedtime each night, but now found himself reading the same page over and over, seeing and comprehending all the words but unable to recall what any of it meant. He had what is called "cognitive impairment," the inability to think logically or creatively, and feels it was almost two years before he was "back on stride" mentally.

I'd been a published writer since before I married Tom, but after his death I couldn't write anything beyond letters and emails to friends, pouring out my heart. One day a magazine arrived with a story I'd written, a light, funny romance. I read it over with wonder. Had I really written that? Could I ever write that well again? I made myself continue going to writers meetings, and eventually I did write and publish again. I'd also traded stocks online, and during the first months after Tom's death I couldn't concentrate on anything as mundane as stocks, and missed out on selling some stocks at a profit.

Connect with Others

Talking things over with others in your situation helps. If there is no counselor or support group available where you live, form your own. There are others like you out there, hurting as you are. Ask at church or in clubs you may belong to. If your spouse was in the military, you have a ready-made support group. If you have children, join Parents Without Partners. If you prefer to chat with others online, there is a website you may find helpful, http://groups.msn.com/ForWidowsOnly.

Try to get back into social activities. If someone invites you to dinner, accept, even if you don't feel like it. Attend the meetings of clubs you belong to. Go to family events such as weddings and graduations, and to your college or high school reunions. You need to maintain connections with others who care about you, and to forgive those friends who don't call you. Some people are like that. You may have to reach out, to make the first moves instead of waiting for someone else to contact you.

Healing takes time. Rosalie wrote from Kenya, "It took me a long time to tick the 'widowed' box on official forms without suffering major pangs. I found the waves of pain and desolation far stronger than I would have believed. After almost five years, they occur less frequently, but are triggered by the most random things.

"Being unable to share something enjoyable is terribly frustrating. Conversely, when something dreadful happens, I feel relieved that he is not witnessing it."

When Healing Doesn't Come

What if you just can't seem to "snap back"? You may be suffering from depression, which goes beyond normal grief. How do you tell the difference?

Many of the symptoms of depression are the same as the characteristics of grief, only exaggerated. You may feel depressed after your loved one's death, but clinical depression goes beyond this.

Here are some signs of clinical depression:

- Thinking or planning of suicide

- Feeling helpless or powerless ("There's nothing I can do")
- Feeling hopeless ("I can't go on")
- Feeling worthless ("There's nothing to live for")
- Lack of interest in doing pleasant things
- Extreme fatigue (Sleeping many hours every day)

If you are suffering from any of these, you should seek professional help from a psychiatrist or counselor.

For most of us, however, grief will ease and a day will come when you will once again enjoy attending a concert, laughing at a joke, seeing beauty in nature or art, playing with your children or grandchildren, sharing the company of friends, and recalling memories of your beloved. You may even love again.

CHAPTER 21
OTHER MATTERS

A marriage doesn't end just because one partner has died. Besides the children, and the memories, there are still many strings tying you to your spouse. You've taken care of legal matters, seen that the will was registered and the estate settled, changed the titles to property and made sure that your deceased mate does not vote absentee. There are still more tasks facing you as you dismantle the symbols of your life together.

Saying "Thank You"

 Write thank-you notes to everyone who sent, did or provided anything to acknowledge your loss.

While those printed cards that say "thank you for your gift" are better than nothing, they're not much better. This is an occasion for hand-written notes. Buy some plain, tasteful notepaper with matching envelopes, and write with blue or black ink.

You need to write these notes yourself. It's not a job to pass on to whoever offers to help. To whom do you write them? To people who have sent flowers, brought food, helped out with chores or donated in the deceased's memory to the charities you designate. You may also write a short appreciative note to friends who wrote you personal notes. It's not necessary to respond to sympathy cards.

And not everybody appreciates sympathy cards. One friend and his wife had taught in Africa on the same project with me. After her death, he sent us a joint annoyed email: "Stop sending me those expensive cards. You're just making the card companies rich, at $5 a card. Give that money to African education. It's what she would have wanted, and what I want." I wrote him a note, glad I'd been too busy to send one of "those cards."

What do you say in your note? Mainly, mention the specific thing you are thanking someone for. "Thank you for your generous contribution to the animal shelter. It was a charity she supported and volunteered at. I'm sure your contribution will be put to good use." Or, "Thank you for bringing the chicken casserole. It was delicious and added to the dinner the family had the night before the funeral."

Try to find out what the relationship was between the donor and the deceased. On two occasions I sent contributions along with a personal note, in one case saying that Tom had been a colleague of Jim and had respected his legal ability; and in the other reminding the daughter of the deceased that I had been her father's secretary and had liked him and his wife very much.

No one read either of my notes, apparently. In Jim's case, the note said how much he had cared for me and other church members, but I was not a member of his church. The boss's daughter apparently had someone else write her thank-yous. She referred to me as "Mrs. Cantieri," instead of "Emilee," which she'd called me when she'd dropped by her father's office and chatted with me, or when I'd been invited to family dinners.

A group thank-you note on the bulletin board at work is not sufficient, unless a collection was taken and a joint flower arrangement or contribution was made, without individual names.

I was told that the choir—to which Tom and I had belonged for years—would handle the reception after his service. Later I learned that several choir members had been joined by my fellow AAUW members, so I found out the names of those who had actually helped and wrote individual notes.

Writing all these thank-yous may seem tedious and over-whelming, but it can be an exercise in gratitude, as you remember and acknowledge everyone who helped or honored your loved one.

Prepare a message for distant friends and acquaintances who may not have heard of the death and make photocopies of the obituary to include. It's okay to send this news by email instead of by personal note, if you know the person frequently checks email.

Tidying Up Accounts

 Remove the name of the deceased from various places.

 If you have not already done so, notify all the doctors who had the deceased as a patient, as well as college alumni groups and associations.

 Cancel magazine and newspaper subscriptions, and send printed forms taking the deceased off mailing lists for catalogs and brochures.

In one day I sent out 42 such notices, tearing off the cover of the catalog or advertisement and attaching a printed notice that said, "Please delete from your mailing list and make no further use of this information." Some catalog companies and charities are very persistent, however. Solicitations still arrive from charities for the former owner of my present house, who has been dead at least seven years.

Arrange to transfer any frequent flyer miles the deceased may have had to you. These are, after all, of value. If you followed the suggestions in the early chapters of this book, consult your list for the correct numbers.

Two of the airlines Tom had accrued miles with were quick to transfer the miles to me after I sent a copy of the death certificate, and one even expressed sympathy. One airline replied that it was not possible to pass the miles, since this could only be done as a gift by a living person, accompanied by a $100 fee. I waited a month, then using Tom's frequent flyer number, I requested that miles be transferred to me as a gift, and put the fee on the airline's credit card. The transfer went through, though Catherine chided me: "Mom, you've got to quit pretending to be Dad."

I suggest you have a friend call each airline and inquire what the procedure is for transferring miles or points. This is a task you can delegate to anyone who asks, "What can I do to help?" That way, there will be no connection to you when you later apply.

I had a task most will not: trying to collect from Access America, the travel insurance company, for the cancelled flights and cruise that Tom and I never got to take. Their rep inquired, "You canceled your trip because a family member died?" "Not just a 'family member,'" I answered, "but one of the travelers, my husband." The insurance company wanted to send the refund to Tom's credit card, which I had already canceled, but eventually and reluctantly sent me a check.

 Check incoming bills to make sure they are legitimate.

I had a question about one from a jewelry store, and called

the store to ask. Tom had taken his father's pocket watch in for cleaning and repair, and it needed to be picked up and paid for. I did both.

With each note, each time you have the deceased's name taken off a list, the death becomes more real, more final. It's difficult to erase someone's identity, but you must do it.

At the same time, you may be commemorating him/her and adding the name to something permanent. If you haven't chosen a marker for the grave, you'll need to do so, and to decide what to have carved onto it.

Since Tom had no grave, Catherine and I donated money for commemorative bricks at the Norfolk Zoological Garden, and Tom's sister Lucy and I had commemorative bricks placed at the college we attended, in memory of Tom and of Lucy's husband Jim, who had died the same year. In addition, the historic cemetery where Tom's ashes are scattered asked that I pay for a shrub to be planted there with a plaque in his memory, and his photo and biography were scanned into an album to be kept there perpetually.

Some people set up scholarships in the name of the deceased, or even donate a building to a college or hospital named for him/her. There are many concrete ways to make sure your beloved is remembered and not just by you.

Checklist for Chapter 21

- ☐ Write thank-you notes to everyone who sent, did or provided anything to acknowledge your loss.
- ☐ Remove the name of the deceased from various places.
- ☐ Check incoming bills to make sure they are legitimate.

CHAPTER 22
LIVING ALONE

Soon after your spouse dies, you will be asked, "What are you going to do now?" Or, "Are you going to stay on here?" (When people asked me that, I'd always think, "No, I'm going off to boot camp. Of course I'm staying here; it's my home!")

Your Home Now

It was the home of you two and probably your children as well. It's now yours alone, to do with as you wish. Imagine for a moment that you have moved to a new house. How would you decorate it? What would you keep, what would you dispose of?

 Make your home your own, reflecting your tastes and interests.

Maybe you were married to a "pack rat" who saved everything. This is your chance to de-clutter. Or maybe your partner was a minimalist so that your home always looked austere and temporary. This is your chance to decorate as ornately as you want. You'll probably want to keep some things that belonged to the deceased, but not everything.

This is the time to get rid of the sagging recliner, especially if you envision your beloved sitting in it. Paint the walls bright cheery colors, and buy a few pieces of new furniture that you really like. Your life is different now, and your home should reflect that.

> Record a new message on your answering machine. Callers who know your spouse is dead may be "freaked out" by hearing the deceased's voice.

My cousin Grace kept her husband's message, including his saying, "this is Larry Gallagher," on her answering machine for several years, until I told her I wasn't going to call her anymore. Finally she got her son to record an outgoing message.

I kept Tom's voice on for perhaps two months. Then Catherine said she wanted to take the recording so she could always remember how her dad had sounded, and she recorded a new message for me.

Clothing

> Begin by getting rid of the deceased's clothing, eyeglasses and hobby materials.

If you keep it around too long, it will fade, go out of style or be damaged by moths. If it is in good condition, donate it or even sell at a consignment shop. Tom had just bought a new tuxedo, which he wore only once, and a new dinner jacket that he'd been planning to wear on our cruise. Catherine sold them both on eBay, so some large man got to wear great-looking clothes for Christmas and New Year's Eve parties.

I was fortunate that our church organist's husband wore the same size clothes as Tom, so Mills chose what he wanted from Tom's wardrobe, and I was pleased, not saddened, to see some of Tom's clothes at church. Mills would approach wearing a jacket I recognized and ask, "How do you like this jacket with this tie? I think it looks really good, don't you?"

I donated Tom's hobby materials and new pajamas and underwear to a nearby veterans' hospital, his hearing aids and eyeglasses to the local Lions Club, his bowties to a friend who also wore them and his books to the library. He had a huge collection of music CDs, many never opened. These Catherine also sold on eBay. I kept all the albums full of our photos and enjoy looking back at them, recalling happy times. I don't need clothes and things to remember him.

Office

My daughter Catherine Cantieri worked as a professional organizer for a couple of years, during which she helped widows redo their late husband's office. "It's the toughest kind of job I get," she said. "They seem to think if they throw away their husband's papers or lesson plans or whatever, they are throwing away a bit of him."

Her advice is to box up everything except what you need, put it away for a few months before you re-attack the collection. As the organizer, she has found important documents underneath sliding heaps of old greeting cards, expired coupons and other paper debris. Keeping everything can result in a home that looks like a "Hoarders" case, and can keep you frozen in the past.

To Move or To Stay?

I had to go ahead with some of the household renovations Tom had planned, whether I wanted to or not. Several years before, we'd added a glassed-in porch to the rear of our house, with a fireplace on one wall. It was a cozy place to spend a chilly afternoon—except when it rained. The roof was pitched too low, and rain blew in under the shingles. We'd planned to have the roof replaced, and had made an agreement with a neighbor, a Coast Guardsman named Ed who did handyman work on weekends.

Ed said he had a friend to help, and on a Friday afternoon they brought over building materials and stripped off the old roof, despite a prediction of snow and rain. They worked all day Saturday but found rot in the wood. On Sunday the friend didn't show up: it was too cold for him. Ed's wife helped out and they managed to get the trusses up before snow began. They worked until it got too dark and slippery to stay on the roof, then threw a tarp over it all.

When I got up the next morning, snow had covered everything including the porch floor, and sleet had formed a crust on top. I crunched my way out to the storage house for the snow shovel, stepping over unknown mounds of snow-hidden rubble. I could recognize the wheelbarrow and the pipe from the fireplace. I chipped my way back and shoveled about three inches of snow off the indoor-outdoor carpeting (which had definitely been "outdoor" that weekend), shoveled the driveway and cracked 6 inches of ice off the top of the car.

I vowed that before another winter came I would sell the house and move to a condo, so someone else could take care of maintaining things. But I didn't. The porch roof was soon replaced and didn't leak, spring came and I learned to cope alone.

🎇 Take your time deciding whether or not to move.

Unless you've always wanted to move to a different location, perhaps for a better climate or to have less responsibility, don't be too quick to give up your home. When everything else had changed so drastically, at least your home should be a stable, dependable place. You know where the doctors, post office, church and supermarkets are, and don't need the stress of finding everything in a different place. Put off making a decision as drastic as moving to a new home until you feel really sure of what you are doing.

Safety

Safety is a concern for those who live alone. I felt very safe in my home, with military officers and their families living on each side of me and a policeman across the court. Later I moved to a retirement community where neighbors can see each other's homes.

I have an agreement with my next-door neighbor to call each other every morning at eight. We alternate, and if Betty hasn't called by 8:05 on "her" day, I call her. If there's no answer, I get the key to her house and go over to check. She has a key to my house, as do two other neighbors, and we've shared our children's phone numbers, in case there is a need for emergency contact.

 Make sure your house is safe, and check your safety measures at least twice a year.

Make sure your outdoor lights work, and if you don't have motion-sensitive lights, install them. Check your smoke alarms at least yearly to be sure they are operative. Have locks on your outside door that must be opened with a key. This will serve two purposes: no one can slip a card into your door to unlock it, and you will not lock yourself out. Give keys to neighbors, but don't hide extras under flower pots or in the usual places. And for locking systems to work, you must remember to lock them. You are on your own now, responsible for your own safety and well-being.

Living Solo

You may have to hire some tasks done and you may need to downsize or "tighten your belt" financially to maintain a home for yourself alone. At least two widows I know had moved with their husbands into a retirement complex, downsizing and making joint decisions about which items to take to the new home. The widows were thus already established in a new place and were not faced with wrenching decisions about moving and dismantling a lifelong home at the same time they were grieving. You can't go back and make this decision, but you can learn to take care of yourself in a new place, or in the old, familiar one.

If you prepared by following Chapter 2, "Managing the Basics," you're ahead of the game.

> If you're starting out now, buy yourself a simple cookbook, especially if it's "Cooking for One," and a tool kit.

This should include a hammer, a pair of pliers, a convertible set of screwdrivers (or three sizes each of flat-head and Phillips-head screwdrivers), a steel retractable measuring tape, an adjustable wrench and a roll of heavy-duty duct tape. As you get more used to doing chores, you may branch out to a power drill. Go back and read Chapter 2, and ask for help with unfamiliar tasks and tools.

Many single people—widowed, divorced or never married—live alone, and most enjoy it. I do. I don't have to clean up anyone's clutter but my own, I can eat when and what I choose, and if I want to stay up all night reading a book, there's no one urging me to turn out the light and get to sleep. I will always miss Tom, as a loving husband, but not as someone to keep me from being lonely.

Rosalie wrote that she found herself becoming more self-centered. "I no longer have to consider Peter's feelings or wishes. I can listen to the same symphony over and over, if I wish." She also finds that friendships have changed since her husband's death. "Some friends that *we* were close and chummy with are no longer bosom chums now that it is just *me*, and others (some of whom had been mere acquaintances before) have become much more important."

Frieda, whose husband was in ill health for several years, found traveling alone after his death to be very different. Before, she'd tried to arrange tours or outings that wouldn't tire him, and when they flew, she'd arranged for help getting him through airports and onto planes. "I always wanted to make sure he was having a good time," she said. Now she could do and see just what she wished.

Frieda and her husband had taken a trip for their anniversary each year, and she decided to continue this instead of sitting home alone remembering. "I am so thankful I did that," she wrote. "It was wonderful. I went to a place we had been together. I did not tell anyone I met that it was my anniversary. I was fortunate that in the group there were other independent travelers as well as couples. The following year I also booked a trip on the anniversary, and that time I told my new friends that it was my anniversary. They drank a toast and I felt celebratory in a good way. This year I have again booked a trip, but will be home the day before my anniversary and will be ready to celebrate here alone. It's strange that what I need as the years go by is different every year."

Checklist for Chapter 22

☐ Make your home your own, reflecting your tastes and interests.

☐ Record a new message on your answering machine.

☐ Donate the deceased's clothing, eyeglasses and hobby materials to people and organizations that can use them.

☐ Take your time deciding whether or not to move.

☐ Make sure your house is safe, and check your safety measures at least twice a year.

☐ If you're starting out now, buy yourself a simple cookbook, especially if it's "Cooking for One," and a tool kit.

CHAPTER 23
GOING ON ALONE

Well-meaning friends—often those who have never experienced the death of a spouse—are full of advice: "Don't make any big changes too soon"; "Pull yourself together"; "Time will make it easier"; and the almost insulting, "You'll find someone else," as if your beloved was as easily replaced as a broken dish.

Based on my own experience, here are some suggestions for going on alone:

1. Decide which portions of your previous life you want to continue with.
2. Maintain your health, safety, property and friendships.
3. Find new activities that will engage you.
4. Don't be too quick to get into a new relationship.

Some of these I followed, some I didn't.

Adjusting to Singlehood

The same friends and relatives who soon after the death didn't want you to be alone, presumably because you might "do something drastic," now leave you alone and return to their own routines. If you have children living at home you will not be alone physically, but you are alone in decision-making, in tasks that you once shared or that the deceased handled. And you have to find a new way of life, depending on yourself.

When I mentioned the difficulties of adjustment to a never-married friend, she said, "Welcome to my world. I've always had to take my car for servicing, prepare my tax return, call the repairman and do everything else that it takes to keep my life and my house running." But it's not the same. As a couple you were used to sharing and dividing and now you are on unfamiliar ground.

The kind of life you led before the death has everything to do with the way you adjust. If you were independent and busy, doing alone some of the things you enjoyed that your spouse did not, you can be independent and busy as a single person.

When Jerry's wife died, he considered what had been "my activities, her activities and our activities. I had to decide which ones I wanted to continue." Jerry, a retired professor, was active in civic and church associations and he planned to keep on with those, perhaps even get more involved, to become "too busy to feel sorry for myself." His wife had been an artist and had quilted and done needlepoint.

"Our joint activities were mainly social," he said. "We had regular evenings out with friends, and they encouraged me to go on with these evenings, even though I was a single among couples. I even took on some of her activities. I pieced together a king-size quilt she'd bought the fabric for and I hired someone to put on the backing and quilt it." Gradually he gave away needlework and art supplies, making his home "his" instead of "ours", though he kept her paintings and quilts.

Tom didn't like to travel, though we did take several overseas trips together, so I had traveled alone or with friends. He made it easy for me, looking after the house and pets while I was gone, taking me to the airport and meeting me, as eager to see me as I was to see him and to share our news and adventures we'd had while we were apart.

The first trip I took alone after his death, I hired the neighbor's twins to look after my dog and cat, but I had to get myself to the airport for an early morning flight. I almost got wiped out by a tractor trailer in the darkness, but I managed to get to the airport parking garage and make my flight. On my return, I walked quickly down the arrival hallway as I had always done, looking for Tom to wave and smile, but there was no one to meet me. I was on my own, and would be from now on.

When Tia's husband knew that his illness was terminal, he planned a trip for her, without him. He made reservations at a motel several hundred miles from their home and insisted that she go for the weekend. She had to gas up the car, check the tire pressure, drive to the distant city, check in, and entertain herself by going to museums, seeing films, whatever she found to do.

"It was a sobering lesson on how I would fare on my own," she said later. "It made me appreciate him while I could still tell him so, and too, after he died I knew I could make trips on my own."

The Little Things

Minor yet significant decisions you'll make are how to refer to things once shared with the deceased spouse, when to stop wearing your wedding ring, and what to say when you meet people who don't know of your spouse's death.

After Tom's death, I had to pause and think when I referred to my home as "ours." I lived alone. There was no one else there to make it "ours." "Our daughter" or "my daughter"? Gradually I realized that I was categorizing things instinctively. Anything that had happened in the past was ours: our trip to Italy, our house in Michigan, the rental property we had bought and sold. Anything that I alone owned or that had been acquired since Tom's death, was "mine," and now when I talk with people who never knew Tom, I refer to "my daughter."

In times past, widows often remarried very soon after the death of a spouse. Those who didn't remarry wore their wedding bands until their own death. Men usually didn't wear wedding rings. Now both parties do, and after a death have to make a conscious decision about continuing to wear the rings. There is no set rule to follow. One widowed man had his and his late wife's rings fused and wore the combined ring. Jen, who started dating her late husband when they were in high school and never loved anyone else, will probably wear her wedding ring as long as she lives, just as widows of the past did.

Some people bury the dead wearing wedding rings and other jewelry. Tom was helping move furniture the day he died and was not wearing his wedding ring, but had left it at home in the jewelry box. I still have it, engraved with our initials and wedding date, as my own is. Since it is gold, I could sell it for a high price, but I can't bring myself to dispose of it.

About four months after his death I went to a family luncheon without my own wedding ring, and my sister noticed and commented. "I'm not married anymore," I answered. I have not worn it since. I've heard that some widows, especially those who travel for business, wear their wedding rings to subtly avoid unwanted advances and keep discussions on a business level. What you decide about wearing your wedding or engagement ring is your personal decision. Do what feels right for you.

The first time I met Jerry, at a social function, he was alone, outgoing, smiling, interesting—and wearing a wedding ring. I wondered where his wife was, and discovered that she had been dead for almost three years. Later, when we started dating, he still wore his wedding ring, but eventually put it aside for safe-keeping. Everyone's pace is different.

Dating

Your social experience may be different from Jerry's: couples may feel uneasy around you, for your presence as a single person is a reminder that they too may soon be widowed. Some of your friends may try to "fix you up," arranging dates for you. Or, if you are a widow, wives may suspect you of trying to attract their husbands.

The solution is to meet new people and make new friends. Take a college class in a subject that interests you. You'll meet people who share your interests. Volunteer at a charity or a fund-raising event. Sign up for a singles cruise. Several cruise lines still offer single cabins, though they cost more than half a double, and some websites have a "singles discount" link. Click on that and you'll see a listing of cruises that have low or no single supplements.

People won't come beating on your door. You must get out in the world and do something. If you are an interesting person, and interested in others, you will find friends—and possibly a new spouse, if you want one.

How soon after a mate's death should one begin a new relationship? Horror tales abound about recently bereaved people who are taken advantage of and stripped of their life's savings, wooed by a clever con artist. It's easy to fall for someone who lavishes praise and gifts on you when you may be feeling lonely and unloved. Take it easy before making any huge step. Unfortunately, wisdom does not automatically come with age, and mistakes are costly.

In spite of all the progress women have made, in many marriages the wife "takes care" of her husband. Bereaved men are usually quicker to remarry than are women, sometimes looking for someone to take care of them as their late wife had done. And because of the disparity in the number of men and women who are widowed, it's a "buyer's market" for men.

Jeremy reported that on his birthday the year after his wife's death, he received ten cards from women—many of whom he didn't know were even aware of when his birthday was. At his high school reunion, he was pursued by several single women from his class who hadn't wanted to date him back in high school, but did now.

Hal and Sylvia shared their grief and began spending a lot of time together. Within six months, to their children's dismay, they announced their plan to marry. When a friend asked Hal, "Do you love Sylvia, or is she just a substitute for Dina?" Hal had second thoughts. He suggested a one-year "cooling off" period, to which Sylvia agreed. She accepted a job in a city one hundred miles away, and moved. They have seen each other several times on weekends, but only as friends. They both have discovered that they like living alone.

Bruce was not as cautious as Hal. Within a year of his wife's death he moved back to his hometown and married his teenage girlfriend. The marriage floundered within six months.

Red Flags

There are warning signs that you are getting involved too soon after your spouse's death, but most of us ignore them, telling ourselves that we know what we're doing.

Widows sometimes remarry out of economic necessity, just as in the old days, and people are curious about others' money. Two men offered to help me with my "investments." I thanked them and told them I already had a financial adviser. A woman friend took me out to lunch and inquired brazenly, "Did Tom leave you well fixed?" "No," I said, "but we together did." Another friend told me solemnly that my friends were "worried" that I might not be okay financially. This was her way of finding out what my financial status was.

Women who are not in financial difficulties often feel free after they get past the initial shock and grief of a death. Having spent years taking care of others, they no longer have to cook, please someone, keep to another's schedule. They can travel, try new hobbies and, in the current phraseology, "reinvent themselves."

Some widows change their appearance, trying out colors and styles the deceased might not have liked. Some get a dog, or take flying lessons, or dance lessons. Dee met her second husband when she broke out of her isolation and took dancing lessons. She had loved dancing in her youth, but her late husband was badly injured in an accident and couldn't dance. I made a solo trip to Tahiti, taking a luxury cruise and going parasailing.

Neither sex should rush into a new relationship. You're too vulnerable and needing comfort at this stage. As Bill expressed it, "You are like the duckling that has just pecked its way out of the egg, wanting imprint and bonding with the first thing it sees."

"You have almost instantaneously become a different person, with different needs, and you may find someone who perfectly meets your needs at that moment," he said. "However, you are starting into another changing phase of your life that will last a year or more, and you will not be the same person at the end of the process.

"You may dismiss differences, like politics, religion, where to live, retirement plans, financial status, travel preferences, and on and on, because you are lonely and this person is available. A year or so later, when you have decided how to live the rest of your life, some of these differences may loom as big mistakes."

Counselors tell divorcing clients that the first relationship after a divorce will end badly—it's just a transition. This is even more so for widows and widowers.

Tony and Carolyn—both widowed—rushed into a relationship too soon. They'd dated in college but had gone their separate ways, keeping in touch mainly through holiday greetings and seeing each other along with their spouses at college reunions. It was at a college reunion after both were widowed within a short time that they re-connected. They reminisced about happy memories of their spouses as well as of college days, and after they returned to their respective homes, they began emailing and phoning each other.

The next step was visiting each other's homes. When Carolyn visited Tony, he took her to restaurants his late wife had liked, and arranged an outing with a couple who had been his late wife's best friends. His house was still filled with her belongings, and her portrait hung over the mantel. When Tony returned the visit, Carolyn showed him a plaque honoring her late husband, and they attended church where Carolyn's husband had been the minister. Tony and Carolyn told each other that they were being open about the past. In fact, they were not ready to say goodbye to their beloved mates. They married, but soon divorced.

I too remarried too soon, only two years after Tom's death. We moved to a new place, away from his home and mine, but our personalities were too different and we had each become, as Bill said, new and different people. After two years we separated and divorced. He is now living across the continent and has formed a new, more satisfying relationship, and so have I.

Give It Time

Widowed people need to get used to being alone and to taking time to let their new being develop. There's no use wondering "What if—" or thinking "If only—". The past is over and the circle that included your beloved mate is closed. You are now part of a greater circle, with potential for change.

I am happy in my present state, remembering the good in the past, enjoying each day, and looking forward to an unknown but undoubtedly interesting future.

This will be the toughest time of your life, but you can go on in a positive manner, being yourself, accomplishing whatever you are intended to do, as your beloved spouse would have wanted you to do.

BIBLIOGRAPHY

Books, Magazines and Newspapers

American Bar Association, *Guide to Wills and Estates* (second edition). New York: Random House, 2004.

American Bar Association Public Services Division, "Health Care Powers of Attorney," 1990.

Anderson, Patricia, *Affairs in Order: A Complete Resource Guide to Death and Dying*. New York: Macmillan & Company, 1991.

Brody, Jane, "Time Enough for a Good Death," *Times News*, Hendersonville, NC, Nov. 8, 2006, p. 2E.

_____, "Living Will Should Spell Out Specifics," *Times News*, Hendersonville, NC, Nov. 9, 2006, p. 3E.

Cantieri, Thomas B., LLM, "Who Needs a Will?", an unpublished article, 2002.

Crenshaw, Albert, "Medical privacy rules complicate planning," *The Virginian-Pilot*, Norfolk, VA, July 14, 2004, page D1.

Demott, John, "The High Cost of Dying," *AARP Bulletin*, October 2009.

"Don't be an heir-head, use estate planning," *The Virginian-Pilot*, Norfolk, Virginia, Jan. 22, 2004, p. D1.

"Don't Forget to Pass on Passwords," Newsletter of Oast & Hook, Portsmouth, VA, Oct. 5, 2007.

"Essential Advisor," brochure by AIG VALIC, Winter 2007.

Haley, James, ed., *Death and Dying: Opposing Viewpoints.* Farmington Hills, MI, Greenhaven Press, 2003.

Herman, Tom, "Digging Out," *The Wall Street Journal*, July 9, 2007, p. R6.

Hyde, Steven L, HFM Investment Advisors, Inc., Newark, DE, telephone and personal conversations 2004-2011.

McNamara, Kristen, "Lights, Camera…Last Words," *The Wall Street Journal*, Dec. 3, 2009.

"Planning Ahead," an interview with professional organizer Maggie Watson, *Times News*, Hendersonville, NC, Jan. 21, 2007, p. 2D.

"Preparing for the Final Hours," *The Wall Street Journal*, Aug. 18, 2009, p. D2.

Silverman, Rachel Emma, "Inheritance Planning without Grief," *The Wall Street Journal,* May 27, 2006, p. B1.

"Good Boy," *The Wall Street Journal*, Dec. 17, 2007, p. R6.

Simpson, Sheila, *The Survivor's Guide,* Toronto, Canada: Summerhill Press, 1990.

Ward, Jessica B., *Food to Die For—A Book of Funeral Food, Tips and Tales.* The Southern Memorial Association and Old City Cemetery, Lynchburg, VA, 2004.

"What Records to Keep and How Long to Keep Them," newsletter, Oast & Hook, Portsmouth, VA, April 13, 2011.

Young, Gregory, *The High Cost of Dying: A Guide to Funeral Planning.* Prometheus Books, Buffalo, NY, 1994.

Online Sources

http://articles.moneycentral.msn.com. "14 mistakes not to make with your will," by Liz Pulliam West, Oct. 1, 2007.

_____ "Who will take care of your kids when you die?" Oct. 1, 2007.

_____ "8 Ways to leave a mess for your heirs," Sept. 20, 2009.

_____ "Your 5-minute guide to estate planning," July 16, 2009.

http://finance.yahoo.com/taxes. April 20, 2011.

http://health.msn.com/health-topics. June 15, 2009.

http://www.nolo.com/article. "Keeping Track of Secured Places and Passwords," by Melanie Cullen, Jan. 3, 2007.

32312371R00120

Made in the USA
Middletown, DE
30 May 2016